# PRAISE FOR *BE YOUR OWN SULTAN*

*Be Your Own Sultan* is more than a book—it's a shift in consciousness. Sultan Batterjee reminds us that true wealth is not measured in material terms but in joy, purpose, and inner peace. As someone who has studied happiness deeply, I'm moved by the clarity this work offers: When we change our mindset, we change our reality. This is a powerful call to step into abundance—not by acquiring more, but by becoming more.

**—Mo Gadwat,**
*author of* Solve for Happy: Engineer Your Path to Joy

This is not a book about money—it's a book about joy. Sultan Batterjee redefines wealth not as a number in a bank account, but as a state of being. *Be Your Own Sultan* invites readers to experience abundance as a way of life—generosity, purpose, creativity, and connection. If you want to live richly, from the inside out you will love this book.

**—Marisa Peer,**
*author of* I Am Enough

*Be Your Own Sultan* is a profound journey into the heart of true abundance. Sultan Sobhi Batterjee offers not just a redefinition of wealth, but a spiritual framework for joyful living grounded in authenticity and purpose. This book is a timely reminder that fulfillment begins not in accumulation, but in awareness. It is a powerful guide for anyone seeking to align outer success with inner peace.

**—Deepak Chopra,**
*author of* The Seven Spiritual Laws of Success: A Pocketbook Guide to Fulfilling Your Dreams

# BE YOUR OWN SULTAN

SULTAN SOBHI BATTERJEE

# BE YOUR OWN SULTAN

## *The* TRANSFORMATIVE POWER *of* REDEFINING WEALTH

Forbes | Books

Published by Forbes Books, Charleston, South Carolina.
An imprint of Advantage Media Group.



Printed in the United States of America.

10 9 8 7 6 5 4 3 2 1

ISBN: 979-8-88750-321-9 (Hardcover)
ISBN: 979-8-88750-322-6 (eBook)

Library of Congress Control Number: 2025900304

Cover design by Lance Buckley.
Layout design by Ruthie Wood.



09-29-2025 11:2

*I've been fortunate in life, but I'm most grateful for all of those who fill every day of my life with an abundance of joy and true wealth: my wife, my children, my mother and father, my sisters and brothers, my family and friends, and my corporate leadership teams and work family. This book—and all that I do—is for all of them.*

# CONTENTS

# ACKNOWLEDGMENTS

One of the most important lessons I've learned is that living a fulfilling life is not a solitary event. It takes a team.

I've built teams at the heart of each of my enterprises, but there are too many people to thank individually. My gratitude goes out to each and every one of them, particularly those in top leadership positions who share my purpose, passion, values, and commitment to the clients and communities we serve.

Recently, I've traveled the world on a journey of personal growth to discover the nature of true wealth. I've met some incredible individuals along the way—a special word of thanks to the one and only Tony Robbins and everyone on his fantastic team, as well as the enlightening Deepak Chopra. The Entrepreneurs' Organization and Young Presidents' Organization have both played pivotal roles in my personal growth and development as a CEO and corporate leader. I'm deeply grateful to all of my fellow members and the officers and administrators of these dynamic organizations. I also thank Adam Witty, everyone at Forbes Books, and my team members who helped me bring my vision to the page and share it with the world.

I'm fortunate to have several friends who've been by my side since we were boys. I hope they realize how much their friendship will always mean to me.

Many mentors have shaped my career and life, but my father has always been a supreme source of guidance and inspiration. My mother is also a strong presence in my life, and I'm grateful for the love and care she's always shown me. I owe my parents a very special debt for everything they've done for me. My family means the world to me, and my deepest gratitude goes to my brothers, sisters, aunts, uncles, cousins, nephews, and nieces.

My eternal thanks to my wonderful wife: my friend, confidante, soulmate, and life partner. I have no words for all she's brought to my world and for being a wonderful mother to my beloved daughter and sons, who were a major inspiration for writing this book. I pray this will be their blueprint for creating lives filled with an abundance of joy.

Finally, when I began this project, I wanted to create something timeless for the great-great-grandchildren and descendants I'm not likely to ever meet. So, for all who follow my line, this book is my gift to you—with the deepest hope that you'll live a life filled with Joy-Wealth and that you'll always be your own sultan.

# PROLOGUE

## The Long, Dark Night of the Soul ... and the Dawn That Follows

Welcome to the New Millennium.

Many bright minds view this era as one in which the greatest challenges will be found in interactions between humans and technology. Artificial intelligence and machine learnings. Virtual reality. Cybernetics.

Others believe our most significant potential lies beyond the bleeding edge of more biological discoveries. Biohacking. Longevity and active ageing. Nootropics. Gene therapy.

While I'm fascinated by and following all of these breakthroughs, I'm convinced the most significant human development in this era will be in the challenges we face within our own humanity. In particular, I believe there's a transformative power to be gained by unraveling a conundrum that's long troubled generations and continues to frustrate even the highest achievers.

Consider the bargain offered to so many of us: Work hard. Get rich. Be happy.

It's a simple proposal—and one that many of us have eagerly accepted.

From entry-level positions to the top of the corporate ladder, we've all worked hard to take full advantage of that bargain.

In fact, those of us in corporate leadership are working harder than ever. A *Harvard Business Review* study showed CEOs work a weekly average of 62.5 hours.[1] That number strikes me as conservative, especially with all of the nonwork we have to contend with: those "immediate attention required" emails, WhatsApp messages, and texts. The online transactions and global commerce. Today's CEO is on duty 24/7/365.

However, it's not just top executives who are working crazy hours.

For those working their way up the corporate ladder, the operative word is *work*. There's little hope of gaining the boss's attention if they're not exceeding the boss's hours.

Even those who've left traditional corporate paths for their own alternative enterprises will find entrepreneurialism is no exception to the demands of hard work.

All of that extraordinary effort must be paying off because collectively, we're getting richer too. There are more millionaires than ever before, and a new billionaire joins those exclusive ranks every day.[2]

Across the board, personal consumption and living standards have increased dramatically.

---

1 Bryan Collins, "How to Work Like a Successful Fortune 500 CEO," *Forbes*, March 14, 2021, www.forbes.com/sites/bryancollinseurope/2019/03/14/how-to-work-like-a-successful-fortune-500-ceo/?sh=7342b7be7498.

2 Alex Morell, "There Are More Billionaires Than Ever Before — and They're Worth a Total of $7.7 Trillion," Business Insider, August 8, 2016, www.businessinsider.com/more-billionaires-than-ever-before-2016-8.

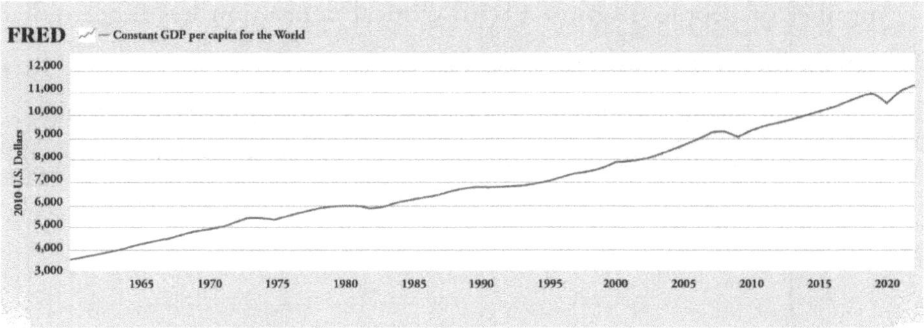


*Figure 0.1: For decades, the global GDP has continually risen over time. Source: FRED, "Constant GDP per Capita for the World," accessed May 2024, https://fred.stlouisfed.org/series/NYGDPPCAPKDWLD.*

Admittedly, there are certain considerations in any economic analysis, but collectively, we're spending more money and enjoying a historic lifestyle that continues to improve.

If we're all working harder and our standard of living is rising, then that's two-thirds of our bargain: Work hard, check. Get rich (relatively speaking), check.

But what about the happiness part?

According to the *World Happiness Report*, the global population has undergone a long-term increase in stress, worry, and sadness.[3] The World Health Organization found that over 300 million people have severe anxiety that qualifies as a mental disorder.[4] Similarly, the

3 Jennifer Liu, "The U.S. Moved Up in This Year's World Happiness Ranking — Here's Where It Ranks Now," MSNBC, March 19, 2022, https://www.cnbc.com/2022/03/19/world-happiness-ranking-2022-where-the-united-states-ranks-now.html.

4 World Health Organization, "Anxiety Disorders," September 27, 2023, https://www.who.int/news-room/fact-sheets/detail/anxiety-disorders.

number of people diagnosed with clinical depression has increased, and antidepressant use has spiked globally.[5]

While many factors influence happiness, the conclusion remains inescapable: around the world, our level of happiness is steadily declining.

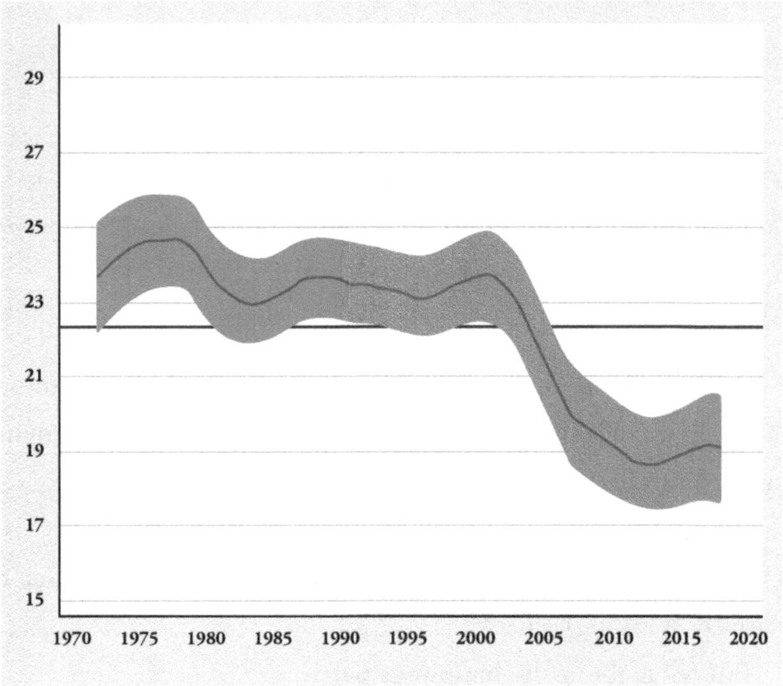


Source: General Social Survey. Population 25 and over, "happy" variable. Scale +100=very happy, 0=pretty happy, -100=not very happy. Sample mean (22.34) shown as horizontal line. Graph shows smoothed mean and 95% confidence interval for each year.

*Figure 0.2: Population happiness has seen a steep and steady decline, particularly in the most recent decade. Source: Sam Peltzman, "The Socio Political Demography of Happiness" (George J. Stigler Center for the Study of the Economy & the State Working Paper No. 331, July 12, 2023), http://dx.doi.org/10.2139/ssrn.4508123.*

---

5 World Population Review, "Antidepressant Use by Country 2024," accessed July 2024, https://www.worldpopulationreview.com/country-rankings/antidepressant-use-by-country.

How does that make sense?

Work hard, check. Get rich, check. Be happy … no.

Maybe the answer can be found by comparing the graph of increasing personal GDP to the graph representing declining global happiness. Overlapping them shows we're working harder and earning more but becoming less happy in the process.

However, there's more than that single indictment here. There's evidence that the traditional concepts of wealth are systemically breaking down. There's no longer any reason to believe that the well-worn paths to success will continue to deliver the same rewards and satisfaction that maybe they once did.

What can be done to reverse this trend of more work and money but less life satisfaction?

That's a daunting question, but I have an answer.

Allow me to set a scene.

We're in the executive suites of a major corporation. The workweek has ended, and all of the offices are dark except for the CEO's. He works twelve or fourteen hours every day, and there's always more work to be done. Business never sleeps, and neither does he.

The lonely hours pass until it's too late to call home without disturbing his wife and waking his children—another lost opportunity to wish them good night. He's missed dinner with his parents too.

He checks his cell phone and realizes he hasn't received a single call. Sure, he knows he's turned down a thousand invitations from friends, but he never thought his lifelong pals would actually stop calling.

The silence is deafening.

He's disappointed but too exhausted to do anything now. His once-boundless energy has faded, and when he does sneak away from the office, he's too tired to enjoy himself. All of this—social isolation, declining health, and a deteriorating mental state—is what he's always thought of as the price of success.

Success is all around him too. He's the head of several companies, all of them flourishing. His office shelves are lined with awards. His family wants for nothing (except time with him). He has all of the trappings of wealth—from watches to exotic cars—and his bank accounts and investment portfolios are formidable.

Still, he's bothered that his cell phone hasn't rung. In that dark moment of the soul, he feels he has everything but lost so much more getting it.

I know this man well ... because he's me.

Or, at least, he *was*.

Not that long ago, I had my own personal existential crisis in which I realized I was a key figure in many lives but disappearing in my own. I felt completely alone.

What I've learned since then is that countless others also bought into the belief that the way to a good life was through working harder, but then discovered this wasn't necessarily the truth.

Are you one of those too?

Do you feel your career requires you to sacrifice everything else? Have you reaped all of the rewards you expected? Or are you, like many others, realizing diminishing returns?

If you are, then you should know I wrote this book for you.

On that night when I realized my phone might never ring again, I swore an oath to find a way to build a joyful, satisfying life.

That set me off on a wonderful adventure traveling the world on a journey of self-exploration, and the lessons I learned fill these pages.

What I have to offer is my philosophy—a means to be truly wealthy and achieve real success by focusing on bringing joy into your life. This revolutionary mindset has revitalized every aspect of my life, including my businesses, and brought positive change to many of those with whom I've shared these thoughts.

The answers you seek are closer than you imagine. In fact, you're holding them in your hands right now.

# INTRODUCTION

## I Am My Own Sultan ... and You Can Be Too

When I was first approached to write a book, I gave the offer serious consideration but ultimately passed. I'd long considered a number of book projects, but my energies at the time were focused elsewhere, and there wasn't a spare moment for anything other than work.

I'd just started my business career and—ever the overachiever—was determined to prove myself through not one but several companies across different industries.

I'm the chairman and CEO of Saudi-based IHCC, a global design and turnkey solution provider specializing in high-performance healthcare, education, and mixed-use development projects in the Middle East and North Africa (MENA). IHCC and all of my companies are industry leaders in delivering high-performance development projects that are focused on positively impacting the communities that they serve. In my role as CEO, I've been recognized by *Forbes* and other authorities as one of the top fifteen CEOs in Saudi Arabia, one of the top ten CEOs in the construction industry, and one of the top one hundred entrepreneurial leaders inspiring the Kingdom of Saudi Arabia in real estate and construction.

I also helm GREENER by IHCC, a professional service provider of resource sustainability and energy efficiency services for buildings and facilities, including consultancy, energy auditing, and commissioning.

In addition, I'm the founder and CEO of Lifestyle Developers, a real estate development company that's an extension of my dream of raising the standards of living and quality of life throughout Saudi Arabia and the entire MENA region. We're a global turnkey solution provider that caters to community members who want to be part of lifestyle destinations by delivering branded residences, lifestyle plazas and gardens, and bespoke hospitality destinations, such as boutique hotels and well-being resorts.

If all that wasn't enough, I'm also a leading executive and board member of Bait Al Batterjee Holding and the Batterjee Foundation, financial entities that strive to address the economic demands of various communities. Furthermore, I sit on the boards of a number of companies, including the Saudi German Hospital Group, one of the largest healthcare providers in the MENA region.

I'd also just started to build a family of my own with my beloved wife and our three wonderful children, and this made me more aware of the significant responsibilities that come with the honor of bearing the name Batterjee.

More than anything, I wanted to wait for inspiration for a book that *needed* to be written.

The intervening years were filled with many successes. My businesses flourished, and my stature in the professional community grew.

I earned accolades and outperformed all of the goals I'd set, reaching a level of success beyond my aggressive ambitions.

Nothing that I've written above is offered as a boast or a brag. Rather, they're the beginning of a humble confession.

You see, I was honored by industry recognition and thrilled by the material rewards of my work, but I couldn't shake the feeling that something in my life was ... well, missing.

I had everything anyone could want, but I felt that life was slipping through my fingers. I should've been on top of the world, but I could feel myself sinking into a dark abyss. That didn't make any sense to me.

I'd done everything I was supposed to do and much more, but my ennui eventually metastasized into disappointment and resentment. Shouldn't I have been rewarded with the happiness and satisfaction I'd been promised?

Hard Work → Success = Happiness

It's a simple equation. So, why did more success bring me less happiness?

As I considered that troubling question, I became aware that I wasn't alone in feeling hollow in the face of abundance. When I looked more closely at my peers, I found that so many of their shiny, happy lives were facades, behind which they were facing the same existential crises that plagued me.

In fact, you may recognize yourself and your own situation. Maybe you understand what it's like to achieve academic accolades, master a profession or two (or more), obtain the highest levels of "success," but still be haunted by the feeling that something in your life is … missing.

In the terrible realization that I wasn't alone in being unfulfilled by my "success," the only comfort was the inescapable conclusion that this experience wasn't mine alone. And, if that was the case, then maybe my disillusionment wasn't a personal failure but a symptom of something far greater—perhaps some defect in our collective mindset. That meant I wasn't broken after all.

That's right: I wasn't broken, and neither are you.

It's simply that the success bargain has become obsolete.

Therefore, I made it my mission to understand exactly what had gone wrong and to find a way to fill my gnawing personal void with something substantive.

In doing so, I also discovered the contents of a book I knew needed to be written.

This is that book—*Be Your Own Sultan: The Transformative Power of Redefining Wealth.*

In these pages, I'll explain how the traditional mindset no longer serves us and walk you through the process of transforming your life by redefining these outdated concepts.

I'll offer you a method for designing your ultimate life and how to plan your goals on what I call the Wealth Pie chart to achieve a life of true wealth.

*Be Your Own Sultan* is my invitation to improve yourself in meaningful and lasting ways and establish independent authority over your life experiences.

The "Sultan" part is a pun referring both to myself and to the traditional title of leadership. I hope the wordplay was clever, but I promise you that neither reference was made lightly.

In the same way that titles are important to books, a person is often defined by their name. When my parents named me Sultan, they gave me no choice but to hold myself to the highest standards of excellence. I'm confident I've lived up to those expectations, and this book is my offer to share my high-achiever mindset.

Of course, the more common meaning of sultan is a title of leadership. From the Arabic *salata*, meaning "to be hard and strong," over the course of time, this came to identify a leader with authority.

At some level, everyone craves some sense of dominion over their lives. *Be Your Own Sultan* was written to offer you the opportunity to establish that sort of control by redefining your priorities, mastering your behavior, and ultimately achieving joy and true wealth.

Keep in mind that the honor of being a sultan carries with it a host of responsibilities. Being your own sultan requires an extraordinary level of commitment to yourself. You can't achieve meaningful change with a few tweaks.

That's where the "transformational power" part of the title enters the equation. This isn't a superficial repackaging but a means for creating a brand-new you. In order to overcome these obsolete mindsets, it's necessary to do the hard work of self-examination and challenge the preconceived notions that limit one's personal growth. You'll need to find a source of strength to power through the process, but if you doubt that you possess such an inner drive, I promise you that through these pages, you'll discover an untapped energy reserve within yourself.

Most of all, what I've written is for everyone, regardless of professional status or position in life. Whether you're a titan of industry or someone just beginning your career, the material in this book will lead you to reexamine the paradigms that constrain you and unlock the door to a personal life experience that offers abundance, satisfaction, and fulfillment.

This book is the guide to being your own sultan.

Before we get started, I think it's equally important to let you know what this book is most definitely *not*.

First, nothing in here is "soft." I'm a businessman grounded in the realities of this world, so when I talk about maximizing joy, that's not touchy-feely. What I've set out is a practical, real-world process for improving your performance in every aspect of your life, including business. Joy is the ultimate goal in building a rewarding life, and that's good business.

Similarly, this book isn't some hippie treatise suggesting we all give up our possessions and worldly ambitions. It's just the opposite. A truly fulfilling life should incorporate every element that provides you joy, and for many of us, that includes professional success, financial security, and material possessions.

This book is not a panacea for whatever ails you or a to-do list that will allow you to check off items and be done. Being your own sultan is a journey, not a destination.

Because of that, this book is not a workbook with the usual exercises and activities. There's no shortage of practical suggestions on these pages, and there are many additional resources available. However, I've intentionally left out the usual homework because I want your initial focus to be on the underlying philosophy.

Finally, this book was written as an invitation to a journey of self-discovery. It's not a doctrine, and I'm no guru. I'm not perfect, and I don't pretend to be. I'm simply offering the lessons I've learned along my journey, including the many mistakes I've made. Finding joy is the most personal of experiences, and how you define those feelings and where you pursue them are a completely individual matter. I only hope that this book can help open your eyes to your limitless potential, inspire you to take up the challenge, and empower you as you embark on the wondrous and rewarding journey.

As a stylistic note, one of my favorite hobbies is watching movies. Action films, dramas, and comedies—I love them all, but I'm particularly fond of documentaries. I've seen *The Last Dance* so many times that I should be the honorary sixteenth member of the 1997 Chicago Bulls, and I'm so fascinated by Dan Buettner's *Live to 100: Secrets of the Blue Zones* that I'm bound to live well past one hundred. Biographies, history, and true life—I relish the opportunity to explore this world and dive deep into myriad subjects through the creative lens of film.

Every day, I strive to live a life worthy of a cinematic retelling. I've tried to capture those same cinematic effects on these pages by creating a reading experience that makes you an active participant in your journey. If my presentation and storytelling strike a spark with you, I hope you'll open your imagination and join me on this very special trip.

So, turn the page, and let's get started.

It's time for you to be your own sultan.

# CHAPTER ONE

## The Beginning

Welcome.

Take a look around us. As far as the eye can see, oceans of sand stretch to boundless horizons in every direction.

You might think we're standing in the middle of a great desert, like *Al robe al Khali* or the Empty Quarter, but it's not like that at all.

Our current location isn't so much a *where* as a *when*.

Everything has a beginning, and this is yours.

This is no actual desert like you'd find on a map. Rather, it's my representation of you—or your consciousness, if you prefer—at your very beginning, when you were nothing at all but could have been absolutely anything. This is you as pure potential: a blank slate.

How did these infinite planes of possibility become the chaotic jungle of thoughts, ambitions, hopes, and fears that you now fight your way through every day? How did you come to be a wanderer searching for purpose and satisfaction in a land that's supposed to be your own—a land that *is* you?

Like most of us, the first construction was likely begun by your parents. They loved you and wanted to give you a good foundation. With the best of intentions, they set down certain standards of conduct and gave you expectations to satisfy. Their hopes for your bright future became a bar for you to clear, a plan you were required to follow, and a path you were expected to walk.

I know something about these sorts of familial expectations. The Batterjees hold Post Office Box #2 in the entire Kingdom of Saudi Arabia, and they've been doing business there proudly since the 1920s, establishing a name brand that stands for honesty, hard work, and community involvement.

Long before I was born, there were pillars in place to shape my upbringing and who I was expected to become. Simply being named Sultan and having the honor of bearing the Batterjee name came with expectations, from my education to my businesses to my personal character.

This isn't a complaint. I'm grateful to all of my family to be able to play a role in such an honored tradition. Still, when you're born into a family of titans, you're expected to be a titan yourself.

While our details may differ, your origin story was also probably written before you were born. Your family wanted a certain life for you and expected you to think and behave a certain way, just like their parents.

On and on, all of us are linked across generations by a long legacy of preconceived thoughts and expected behaviors.

There's nothing inherently wrong with this, but in terms of our opening metaphor—that open plane of your infinite potential—that same area is no longer so limitless. Those endless horizons are now defined by buildings that create skylines, and the paths you might've blazed yourself are now streets and sidewalks with traffic lights and crossing signals.

Welcome to the City of Expectations.

Now, that vast expanse of possibility is crowded with construction. A foreign place not entirely of your making, the City of Expectations can be hostile and difficult to navigate. In the city, you work constantly to meet external demands and navigate a labyrinth built by others.

When I first entered my own City of Expectations, I did great.

I was a successful businessman and had an amazing family and great friends.

Still, I couldn't find an authentic home in the City of Expectations simply because this place wasn't mine. I'd been born with limitless possibilities but lived a life of limits set by others. Rather than building something to meet my desires and aspirations, I'd settled for a prefabricated life that required concessions and accommodations.

How about you? Have you found your home in the City of Expectations?

Or, do you find that no matter how hard you work, you live on someone else's terms without the freedom to be your authentic self?

What I've discovered through my journey is that a life of personal fulfillment is only possible when we act with authenticity. That is, the only way to get what you want is to know what you want and then make those goals your life's pursuit.

Of course, this leaves us with a cumbersome situation. Where you once had a vacant space to build whatever your heart desires, you now have the crowded metropolis of the City of Expectations. There's little room to build anything of your own unless you're willing to clear away what doesn't work and begin building on a completely vacant lot.

If you want to create your own life, you'll first have to clear out your old way of thinking by razing your version of the City of Expectations.

With that in mind, take some time to sit with everything we've covered and give some thought to the external expectations that have limited your thoughts and actions. Consider everything you've done because you felt you had to or because it was the right thing to do. What are your limiting beliefs? What would you accomplish if everything were possible again?

There's no need to hurry through this process. It's better to take your time, because I can't overemphasize the importance of identifying your limiting beliefs and how they control you. To work through this process, you're going to need an open mind, because I'm about to explain that many of those limiting beliefs are based on just one word.

That's right. One word: wealth.

When you're ready, turn the page, and we'll continue.

# CHAPTER TWO

## That Table in the Book Shop

*What do you really want out of life?*

I've asked myself that question a thousand times.

When I first began my journey, I thought that my disillusionment was a reflection of my failures and that the answers might be found by observing all those others who seemed so content. However, I soon discovered that most of those supposedly happy people were wrestling with the same issues I was.

*What do you really want out of life?*

I can't think of a more wonderful place to consider this question than The Romanos, a luxury resort on the Ionian Sea. Imagine yourself here with me, where the warm sea breeze whispers through olive trees and the sun's reflection glows gold on the water where the sky meets the Mediterranean.

Heaven on Earth.

You'd think that if there was any place where you could come up with an answer for what you really want out of life, it would be an idyllic place like this. However, our time here has ended, and we have to rush to get a car back to the airport now.

That's disappointing, I know. I didn't get a chance to enjoy my stay at The Romanos either, because the purpose of my visit was business, not pleasure.

There's a lesson to be learned here.

I have a lot of businesses, and that means a lot of meetings in a lot of different places. I'm frequently shuttling from one city to another, staying at the finest hotels, and dining in the best restaurants—but almost always for business. That may sound exciting, but no matter how amazing the accommodations are, a hotel suite never feels like home. What I usually see in all these capital cities are the routes to and from the airports, just like today.

In fact, now that we've arrived at the airport, I won't even get the chance to fly home. Instead, I'm off to Dubai, London, or someplace in between.

I'm not complaining. Travel is a necessary part of doing business in a global market, and I'm grateful for every opportunity. I'm just suggesting that things aren't always as glamorous as they first appear.

*What do you really want out of life?*

Have you come up with an answer yet?

Let me guess. It's not hard because most people these days tell themselves the same thing: "I want to be rich!"

That's why lifestyle TV is a global phenomenon, social media influencers make fortunes without breaking a sweat, and markets are clogged with day traders and crypto millionaires. Everyone is chasing "The Dream" and that means getting rich.

From the driver who just dropped us off at the airport to the other travelers rushing through the terminal, everyone wants to hit the jackpot.

Did I get that right? Was your answer to the question that you want to be rich?

No judgment. I've been candid about a time when my response would've been the same.

Everybody wants to get rich.

However, let's reconsider our fellow travelers here in the airport for a moment.

I'm not the only one flying for business, and I'm clearly not alone in having reached a certain level of success. Many here are dressed in tailored suits and designer clothes. They carry expensive luggage. With their well-coiffed heads and designer shoes, they're all racing after riches.

Still, I can't help but notice how many of them seem resigned as they grimly make their way along the concourse. I'm sure they're all wonderful, vibrant individuals, but their expressions are dull and their movements robotic. They seem completely joyless.

Maybe I'm so quick to recognize their disconsolate state because I used to be like them. I can't help but recognize all the symptoms of those high achievers who are feeling more and more dispirited.

Consider for a minute a recent Credit Suisse report that found the number of millionaires rose significantly in a two-year period.[6] And there's every indication this trend will continue.

That's a positive development, right?

But then, why have levels of depression and anxiety also skyrocketed during that same period? This trend is also likely to continue.

---

6 BBC News, "Millions Become Millionaires during Covid Pandemic," June 23, 2021, https://www.bbc.com/news/business-57575077.

If more people are getting rich, then why is there a significant uptick in the number of mental health issues evidencing a general dissatisfaction with life?

Let's walk down the concourse, and I'll show you something. Like every airport in the world, we won't have to go far before we find a bookstore. While people are reading less and less, I guarantee there'll be a table in the back piled high with self-help books. Self-help constitutes the largest and most profitable genre of nonfiction publishing in the world, making over $1 billion annually.[7]

I have the greatest respect for self-help books and regularly consume several titles every week. And if you look at the more prominent titles on that table, chances are good that I'm fortunate enough to count some of the biggest names as personal friends. All of those authors are amazing people, doing meaningful work in opening up the human experience to the reading public.

What I'm suggesting, however, is that maybe we readers are missing the mark. Maybe what needs help isn't ourselves but our mindsets.

Three hundred thousand years ago, when our ancestors first emerged on the African savannah, survival was tied to following the other members of their group. If someone broke into a panicked sprint, it wasn't necessary for everyone to see the lion in the tall grass. They all ran to safety together.

In the millennia since then, our instinct for imitation hasn't lessened. We still have a predilection to do what everyone else is doing without thinking much about it.

---

7 Jessica Lamb-Shapiro, *Promise Land: A Journey through America's Euphoric, Soul-Sucking, Emancipating, Hornswoggling, and Irrepressible Self-Help Culture* (New York: Simon & Schuster, 2014).

So, with so many of us focused on getting rich, it's not surprising that the rest of us would join the same mad pursuit even if it might be leading us over a cliff, like lemmings.

I previously introduced the metaphorical City of Expectations and asked you to clear your mind of all those preconceived constructions and limiting beliefs. I hope you've achieved that clarity, because it's time to share with you something that contradicts everything we've been led to believe.

What if the dissatisfaction plaguing so many people isn't a result of *what* they're doing but rather *why* they're doing it? What if it's wanting to get rich for the sake of getting rich that's led us astray?

Hold that thought. My phone is ringing, and I have to take the call.

It's my wife. She's calling to say she misses me and remind me we have a get-together with family this weekend. My eldest son wants to share a story about his day, and my younger boy needs equal time. My daughter has to tell me she can't wait to go swimming with me again. I send them all to bed with an "I love you" and tell my wife that I love her too.

Sorry for the interruption.

Where were we? Oh, that's right, I was telling you that maybe it's a mistake to make your primary objective in life just to get rich. Maybe there's a different kind of wealth we should be chasing.

Rather than riches, I've discovered that it's more important to be truly wealthy—a status not dependent on numbers in my accounts.

With the right mindset, anyone can be wealthy.

Turn the page, and I'll share what you need to know to be wealthy too.

# CHAPTER THREE

## Transforming Your Life ... One Word at a Time

Words.

We type away or speak freely but never give real thought to what words mean and how they work.

I've taken us to another location: a ballroom in a four-star hotel. These spots are the same all over the world. They're utilitarian spaces bounded by sliding wall partitions, with beige commercial carpeting underfoot and paneled ceilings overhead.

I don't need to describe more, because you already know this place, with the unflattering fluorescent lighting and constant hum from the air-conditioning vents.

How could you recognize a room you've never been in?

Words. My description of the location brought to mind your experiences and created a shared connection between us. Our worlds came together with nothing more than a few words.

In the same way, we use words to create connections with the rest of the world. That's the very nature of communication.

However, are those connections accurate and trustworthy?

While words may be the building blocks of our social interactions, self-expression, and shared life experiences, they're open to misinterpretation and are surprisingly inexact for such delicate operations. As my assembled team is about to learn, many words have definitions that can change from user to user and get lost in translation.

Let's turn back to this ballroom we both think we know so well. A couple of days ago, this room might have hosted a wedding reception or a business convention, but today, there are rows of banquet chairs arranged for a team-building event I'm hosting.

I'm in the process of creating a new hotel brand, and I've brought together the top leadership involved in this undertaking so that we can take a brief break from operations and spend a moment strengthening our team, which I believe is just as important to the overall project.

I'm a big believer that there's a tremendous return on investment from developing your teams. Sometimes, I host programs focused on keeping ahead of the curve with the developing technologies in our industry. Other times, my executives focus on self-development with Tony Robbins's amazing corporate training team. Also, I often bring my employees together just to enjoy the camaraderie we share as teammates.

Today, I've brought the leaders of my hotel development team together so we can learn about the power of words.

I want you to think about that too.

Take the word "bold," for example.

Four letters, one syllable—it couldn't be much simpler.

Still, when today's speaker asks my team to think about the word "bold" and share their definitions, the results are surprising.

Some of my executives think the word means "courageous and assertive." That's a quality any leader would want incorporated into their corporate team, right?

However, others feel that the word "bold" suggests someone who's "unruly" and "given to defying established protocols." That sort of potentially mutinous mindset may constitute a considerable liability in corporate C-suites and boardrooms, right?

One word, two different interpretations. One is an asset to your team, while the other is a breakdown waiting to happen.

Of course, both interpretations are correct.

That's the thing about words. There's more than just how they're spelled or pronounced. Languages are alive, and words have an emotional component that's every bit as important as any dictionary definition. It's about how a word makes us feel.

In that regard, I don't think many words—no matter the language—are more emotionally charged than this one: wealth.

When you read that, what did you think?

More important, how did you feel?

For some, no doubt the word conjured up the sweet sensation of answered prayers for the abundance they've already received. Maybe some found a challenge stoking their sense of competition. There were certainly others who felt the terrible ache of jealousy or the bitter stab of rewards always unjustly held out of reach.

Just like the differing definitions of "bold," all of the various meanings that might be assigned to the word "wealth" and all of the emotions they conjure up are completely valid.

Today, most people think getting rich is the same as being wealthy, but that's part of the trap that so many of us have run into head-on. We fall for the deceit that getting rich is the ultimate reward and that there's nothing else we can bring into our lives to make them even more satisfying.

*That's* the big lie.

There's so much more to a satisfying life experience than just getting rich, but everything depends upon the mindset you choose to hold.

Very little of this world is objective and absolute. In fact, your entire life is a matter of perspective. You can view your struggles as insurmountable obstacles or exercises strengthening you for your inevitable success. The criticisms of others can be taken as paralyzing attacks or new insights into steps you might take to improve yourself. Any failure can be seen as a debilitating loss or a learning experience that leaves you better prepared for your next attempt.

I was first exposed to the essential nature of one's mindset by Tony Robbins, who repeatedly explained to me that a person's mental force is largely a determinant of the life they lead. Many people discount how important their mindset is and focus on their practices instead.

"If I do this ..."

"If I do that ..."

It's not that our actions aren't important to our overall success, but by focusing simply on the physical, it's easy to overlook the inescapable truth that it's our mental game—our mindset—that's primarily responsible for our life experiences, including our actions.

Every scenario is different and susceptible to a host of variables, but no matter what you're trying to achieve, mechanics account for around 20 percent of the result, while the remaining 80 percent all comes down to your state of mind.

The perfect example of this is Michael Jordan. We can talk about who was or is the best player in the NBA, but that conversation will always conclude with MJ as the GOAT. No doubt his training regimen was legendary and his game mechanics were extraordinary, but what truly distinguishes Jordan is that his mindset was focused on doing everything necessary to become a champion.

Over the course of his career, he suffered his share of tragedies, setbacks, and losses on the court, but he never once played the victim or collapsed in defeatism. At the same time, with all of his personal accolades and team championships, he never allowed himself to become deceived by his success and fall into thinking that he could let up on his intensity. His mindset was focused on being a champion, and that's what made it possible for a kid who couldn't make his high school team to become the best of the best who ever played the game.

The same is true for you. Your mind must be fixed on doing everything necessary to realize your goals and fulfill your life of Joy-Wealth. Your focus, confidence, and commitment must always be unshakable. If your mindset is weak and opens the door to doubt and second-guessing, then it won't be long before failure creeps in through that opening. If you're willing to entertain the thought that you've already done enough and that it's time to rest, it will be virtually impossible to develop yourself into a champion or live a life filled with joy.

Because mindsets are so important and because words are so powerful but easily confused, I want to be precise about my usage. To that end, I've created several terms of art to capture the precise usage necessary to consider your path moving forward.

I'm not judgmental about any of these mindsets, but I do believe that they reflect varying degrees of personal insights, with one building upon the other. In fact, I believe they can all be placed on a sliding scale that reflects varying degrees of self-awareness and, correspondingly, different potentials for true satisfaction and fulfillment in life.

## The Get-Rich Mindset

The most common mindset is for all of those who think conspicuous consumption and status-bragging are the same thing as wealth. Don't let the name fool you. This mindset isn't about professional success or financial attainment; it's about impressing others and creating a false persona. Ultimately, the real focus here is on satisfying the external demands placed upon us in the City of Expectations by trying to impress others and finding meaning in ostentatious materialism.

This is the mindset that prioritizes the sort of bragging and flexing that drives social media with nonsensical posts of mansions, exotic cars, and designer clothes to pull "likes" from the gullible masses. This is a mindset that's completely dependent on others and reflects a lack of self-esteem, which requires external validation.

The Get-Rich Mindset may create momentary highs, but there's no lasting satisfaction because it's rooted in temporary gratification and external validation. The simple truth of life is that you can't find lasting satisfaction when you live for the approval of others.

## The Material-Wealth Mindset

This mindset reflects a slight elevation in personal development from the Get-Rich Mindset by trading external approval for the intrinsic value in material things and satisfying societal obligations on a personal level. This is the mindset that seeks to meet the burdens of the City of Expectations to satisfy a more personal desire.

I'd be the last person to suggest there's anything inherently wrong with wanting fortune and the first person to attest to the necessity of financial security for you and yours. There's an undeniable pleasure to be derived from obtaining prosperity and possessions, such as a beautiful home, exotic automobiles, luxury travel, and exquisite jewelry. Whatever inspires you, there's real value in bringing items you desire into your life.

Similarly, there's personal satisfaction in fulfilling the societal responsibilities you embrace or achieving professional ambitions. I've found substantial joy in attaining my professional accomplishments, making my parents and family proud, and earning industry accolades.

The key element here is that the Material-Wealth Mindset is focused on these pursuits for personal fulfillment, not the people-pleasing incentive that drives the Get-Rich Mindset. Rather than a flex for others, the Material-Wealth Mindset is concerned with self-satisfaction.

That's certainly an important distinction, but the Material-Wealth Mindset is still unsustainable for providing long-term fulfillment. Whether you're motivated by a public flex or an internal drive, there's no lasting satisfaction to be found in an inauthentic life that doesn't serve your needs and desires.

## The Joy-Wealth Mindset

The Joy-Wealth Mindset is the ultimate goal of all of those who strive to be their own sultans. This way of thinking doesn't attempt to deny the value of riches and position and recognizes that there are additional components that are necessary to round out your life and provide deep and lasting satisfaction. These additional elements are based on the understanding that true wealth can't be bought at any price but instead exists in a pervasive sense of joy within your authentic self—one that isn't dependent on exterior validation or material pursuits. The Joy-Wealth Mindset produces meaningful life experiences by prioritizing, creating, and cultivating joy in every aspect of your life. This sense of joyful abundance is what true wealth is all about.

## Types of Wealth

In addition to the wealth mindsets defined above, let me take this opportunity to define for you two types of wealth in a temporal context.

As we progress through the process of redefining wealth as part of developing a Joy-Wealth Mindset, we'll participate in an exercise in which you'll envision yourself at your eighty-fifth birthday party as a highlight of the dream life that you'd live if you were able to bring all of your aspirations to fruition. The purpose of this is to identify the elements of your life that are most important to you over the projected course of your life.

By examining your life this way—starting at a triumphant point in the distant future and then working backward—you'll be better able to identify what really matters to you. By capturing your perfect life as it expands over time, you'll also come to better appreciate the temporal component of wealth. That is, it will become clear that wealth must be considered on a calendar: What do you have now? What do you want in the future?

**Current wealth** reflects the assets—material and otherwise—that you possess in the present moment.

Think in terms of an audit. Current wealth is what you hold in the present moment. It includes not only your financial possessions but all of the assets that you hold. In this regard, I invite you to make an audit of your current wealth and pay attention to the most important assets you hold.

Are you supported by a loving family and loyal friends? Are you reasonably strong and healthy in your body and mind? Do you have opportunities to continue your education and build your career? Do you have all of the resources that you need?

All of these—your family and friends, your health, and your opportunities—are important assets that you possess in the present moment and of which you should be mindful.

**Forecasted wealth** represents assets—material or otherwise—that you reasonably expect to reap in the future as a result of investments or other future-oriented activities.

In contrast to the audit to account for current wealth, the assets that comprise your forecasted wealth can be best considered by thinking in terms of a business plan.

What would you like your family status to be in the coming years? What are your health goals? What do you wish to accomplish in your lifetime? What do you have now that you want to ensure you'll continue to have in the future?

These unrealized assets that you intend to obtain or achieve in the coming years—a happy family, a strong body, and a flourishing career—constitute your forecasted wealth.

To achieve the Joy-Wealth Mindset, you must focus on current and forecasted wealth simultaneously and keep them relatively balanced throughout your life.

If your attention is focused solely on current wealth as in the case of the Get-Rich Mindset, then you won't have the sort of future-oriented personal investments that are necessary to provide you with rewards as the years progress. If you haven't devoted time to building your family, you may become estranged. If you've neglected your health, you may become sick or infirm. If your time was wasted on your Get-Rich flex, then you probably won't have a career to sustain you as you grow older.

In the same way, if your focus is solely fixed on your forecasted wealth activities, then you'll end up squandering assets in the present moment. If you're working all of the time to build your business in the future, you'll miss out on time with family and friends. If you save every riyal and don't take the opportunity to enjoy yourself from time to time, you may come to the end of your life with substantial savings, but you'll be very poor in life experiences.

Therefore, to be your own sultan, you must always maintain a balance between the two. A sultan is always balancing these two components of true wealth so that they can remain present in the moment but also move forward strategically toward the accomplishment of their goals.

With all of that in mind, has your definition of a wealthy life shifted?

If all of this has been a bit overwhelming, don't worry. We're about to have a good time. I'm about to take you to a very fancy event. That's right. We're going to a soiree.

# CHAPTER FOUR

## If It Makes You Happy, Why Are You So Sad?

I'm not only the head of several global businesses; I'm also deeply involved in a number of charities. So, I get invited to a lot of social events. This one I've brought you to could be any of them.

If you were to ask the catering staff circulating through this crowd, carrying trays of hors d'oeuvres and canapés, I think they'd say that every guest at this event would meet the definition of wealthy. Maybe you would too.

However, I assure you that's not how the guests themselves would see things.

The guests who'd earned their money might not feel wealthy when coming face-to-face with those guests who come from generational dynasties. Millionaires might not feel wealthy making small talk with those worth hundreds of millions. Multimillionaires might become uncomfortable chatting up a billionaire.

To bring our assessment to full circle, there are many others who live at the edges of this or any city who'd consider the hard-working catering staff counting their earnings at the end of the night as wealthy too. Whatever your situation, those people might also consider *you* wealthy.

The definition of "wealth" is dependent on an individual's perspective and isn't as universal as you've been led to believe. Wealth is more a reflection of your mindset than your bank account.

You're wealthy if you think you are.

So many individuals set earnings goals and then pin everything on attaining that level of financial success. "If I can only make *this* much money, then I'll be wealthy."

However, these types of goals are constantly shifting and moving away. There's never a point of satisfaction to be savored. Instead, there's always a new hurdle to clear, and on and on it goes without any satisfaction from reaching the goals we've set for ourselves.

Moreover, reaching these types of life markers doesn't always produce the results most of us expect.

Look around the crowd of guests at this soiree. They look fabulous, laughing and appearing to have a grand time. However, those smiles don't necessarily reflect their real situations. Even with their luxury cars and haute couture fashions, they may still feel unsatisfied with their lot in life—even if you might see their positions as wealthy.

For many of those guests, the demands of business require all of their time. Some may find themselves alone in their mansions with failed marriages or ruined relationships with their children or parents. Others may be plagued by depression and anxiety or have addiction issues or serious health concerns.

In other words, despite what anyone on the outside might perceive as wealth, they're just like everyone else and susceptible to the human issues that are part of every life.

This point was driven home by a Nobel laureate in economics, Angus Deaton, who published a groundbreaking study concluding that any benefit to mental well-being as a result of financial standing balances out at a relatively modest income level. The ability to sustain oneself and one's family is all that's required to achieve peace of mind, and additional money won't necessarily improve one's overall life satisfaction.[8]

Anyone who believes that riches can cure all issues should check out Netflix's excellent *The Billionaire, the Butler & the Boyfriend* (*L'Affaire Bettencourt: Scandale chez la femme la plus riche du monde*), which examines how wealth acted as an accelerant to the bitter feud between L'Oréal heiress Lilianne Bettencourt—once the richest woman in the world—and her daughter.

In fact, money may make life tougher in some situations. A recent report in *Harvard Business Review* suggested that prioritizing money over other considerations undermines personal happiness.[9] Other studies have indicated that wealthier individuals often spend more time engaging in activities that are less enjoyable than the less affluent and report increased anxieties related to time pressures.[10]

---

8 D. Kahneman and A. Deaton, "High Income Improves Evaluation of Life but Not Emotional Well-Being," *PNAS* 38, no. 107 (2010):16489–16493, https://doi.org/10.1073/pnas.1011492107.

9 Elizabeth Dunn and Chris Courtney, "Does More Money Really Make Us More Happy?" *Harvard Business Review*, September 14, 2020, https://hbr.org/2020/09/does-more-money-really-make-us-more-happy.

10 A. Whillans, L. Macchia, and E. Dunn, "Valuing Time over Money Predicts Happiness after a Major Life Transition: A Preregistered Longitudinal Study of Graduating Students," *Science Advances* 9, no. 5 (September 18, 2019), https://doi.org/10.1126/sciadv.aax2615.

Of course, none of this is meant to suggest that affluence can't offer a significant component to overall life satisfaction. At the very least, financial security for you and your family is a necessity. Frankly, lavish events like the one we just attended can be tremendous fun.

My point here is that despite the many advantages and wonderful benefits that may accompany financial prosperity, it's not the magic bullet you've been promised. On the contrary, wealth is a matter of perspective, and unless you open your life to truly meaningful and satisfying possibilities, the Get-Rich Mindset can lead you astray.

# CHAPTER FIVE

## The Shortcomings of the Material-Wealth Mindset

There's something special about throwing off the constraints of land-based living and heading out onto the open water. Boating is one of my great pleasures in life, as the feeling it gives me frees me from my day-to-day troubles and concerns.

Still, if I'm not careful and I chart an errant course, I can quickly find myself lost in dangerous waters and headed toward disaster.

Similarly, focusing your life on the wrong point on the wrong landmark, such as chasing after riches, conspicuous consumption, and financial flexing, can lead you to become dangerously lost.

There are just as many missteps you can make when charting a course in pursuit of riches. This is by no means exhaustive, but the following are some of the most common missteps that can arise from maintaining the Material-Wealth Mindset.

## The Business-Only Focus

Focusing on prestige and riches isn't the same as pursuing career goals and professional ambitions. It's easy to confuse them because when you're starting in the business world, focusing your energies and attention on creating a solid foundation is essential. I'd be misleading you to suggest otherwise.

Still, as much as your business needs your investment of time and energy, there's a considerable catch—one that's subtle and easy to miss.

When I first began in business, I was intent on establishing a reputation that honored the Batterjee name and established me in the industry.

Burning with ambition, I focused all of my energy on this from the time I rose very early in the morning until I went to bed at night—if I slept at all. All I did was work, and my businesses were the primary things on my mind. There was little room in my life for anything else.

Nothing about this seemed selfish to me. On the contrary, my devotion to work wasn't solely about my ambition but an expression of my commitment to my family. When my merciless routine was interrupted for a special occasion, I didn't know how to explain to people that I was distracted by business and consumed by guilt for expending time I could've otherwise spent working.

I love my parents very much, and we've always been extremely close. Nevertheless, my business-only focus turned my regular visits into occasional interruptions in my jam-packed schedule. One afternoon, I tried to make up for my absences, but when I showed up at their door, I was absolutely exhausted and clearly paying a very heavy price for my devotion to business.

Sometimes, the most special people in our lives have a way of understanding a situation and cutting straight to the truth. My mother took one look at me and called me aside. She told me to sit down, and then softly but firmly said, "My son, the work never ends, and you are not your business."

Simple words, but among the most profound I've ever heard.

With the Material-Wealth Mindset, it's easy to become obsessive with your focus on business success. I suppose that kind of mindless ambition makes a twisted sort of sense in that mental state.

Still, my mother's wise words completely exposed the shortsightedness of my commitment. No matter how many hours I chained myself to my desk, there'd always be more work to do. In the end, I wasn't my business. I may have been building up each of these companies, but to do so, I was tearing myself down.

With her simple admonition, my mother gave me one of her greatest gifts and left me with a wonderfully profound question: "If you're *not* your business, then just who are you?"

That question was a major inspiration for my journey of self-discovery and alerted me that I needed to update my perspective before I found myself lost on the high seas of life.

## Competition versus Comparison

Whether in the boardroom or on the football field, I admit to having a strong competitive spirit. Whether I'm negotiating a contract or playing football in the backyard with my kids, I'm not ashamed that I want to win.

I don't see anything wrong with competition because it makes me a better businessman and prepares my children for the world they'll face.

In this way, I don't think competition should be seen as a struggle for domination. Instead, it's a mutually beneficial chance to learn and grow.

But as with other elements, competition can be taken to extremes. When taken beyond reasonable limits, there's a real danger of healthy competition becoming twisted into something very toxic: comparison.

The distinction between the two is subtle but important to mind. Competition's ultimate goal is strengthening and self-improvement, while comparison becomes a descent into jealousy and envy that guarantees disappointment.

Consider a professional football club that takes to the pitch against a squad from a university and comes away with a victory after playing a sloppy game. Have they really won? Sure, they scored more goals, but real success has slipped through their fingers with their subpar performance.

On the other hand, if that same squad of university players gave their very best and exceeded themselves in every aspect of the game, then did they really lose? In the end, they were on the low end of the scoreboard, but if they all managed to play the game of their young lives and exceeded their previous performance, isn't that the ultimate victory?

Being a champion isn't about beating your opponent. It's about outperforming yourself.

Let me clarify the distinction. My extended family has made a long-standing tradition of spending several summer weeks at Marbella, Spain, on Andalusia's Costa del Sol.

One afternoon, some of my family decided to take a tour of some properties for sale. Because architecture and design are both my business and my passion, I was eager to go.

The first property we looked at was a wonderful example of classic Andalusian architecture: beautiful and elegant. This was a perfect home in Costa del Sol, and everyone loved the authenticity and simple design.

The second property had more modern features and amenities and was about twice the size. Suddenly, the first house everyone had just raved about didn't seem as wonderful by comparison.

When we arrived at the third house, we were greeted at the door by the owner, a well-known football coach. This was no mere house, but a veritable castle of glass and steel. The amenities were luxurious, and the views were breathtaking. By any standard, this property was extraordinary.

Afterward, all my companions were focused on the third house. This was undoubtedly a very special property, but I was struck by how quickly they'd forgotten the other two homes, which they'd both loved when they first saw them.

Someone remarked about the football coach, and I observed, "Can you imagine where the *owner* of that football club lives?"

My point here is that no matter where you live, there'll always be someone who lives in a bigger house, a newer house, or a more lavish house. If your Get-Rich Mindset is focused solely on the dimensions of a house and not on the love that fills your home, you'll always be disappointed.

## The Limitless Mindset versus Forward-Fixed Thinking

Of all the negative aspects of the Material-Wealth Mindset, I think the most damaging feature might be the limits it places on one's potential.

We previously discussed my love of boating and the sense of freedom I find on the open water. When all of the edifices on the horizon shrink to nothing, there's nothing to confine you, and life seems limitless. You can measure the distance you travel across the open sea in knots, but it's a difficult and inexact process without fixed landmarks in the distance. Out on the water, life's not about covering a specific distance, but about enjoying the voyage.

For those who are still trapped in the Get-Rich Mindset, their journey in life is necessarily limited by the markers and buoys of external expectations. With those kinds of limits in place, the experience loses the appeal of a sea cruise and becomes more of a slog from slip to slip without the enjoyment of the outing.

For example, if those with these limited mindsets set a goal to make a million dollars or if they want to be able to purchase one luxury item or another and they manage to achieve those significant accomplishments, any satisfaction they realize with their successes can only be temporary and must be replaced with another new goal … and another, and another. It's a relentless cycle.

With the Material-Wealth Mindset, every day comprises chasing another elusive objective. It's this wheel of success that grinds up so many who attempt to create a meaningful life by chasing temporary goals.

Add to this the effects of comparisons that we've discussed, and there's not only another goal to chase but also someone who's already accomplished it and achieved more.

Make a million dollars? There's someone who's made two … or ten or twenty.

Grow your business? There's a business that's bigger or growing more quickly.

Indulge yourself in conspicuous consumption? Someone owns more or better or newer or nicer.

With the Material-Wealth Mindset, there's never an opportunity to appreciate what you have in the present because the focus is always on the ever-elusive future. This guarantees disappointment and dissatisfaction.

Maybe you feel the pressure of running on that wheel that leads nowhere and would like to find a way off. If so, turn the page. We'll keep moving forward toward being your own sultan.

# CHAPTER SIX

## The Mirage of the Material-Wealth Lifestyle

As I've made clear, none of this came to me as a philosophical abstract. I've not only had the Material-Wealth Mindset—I've lived the life that comes with it. That life was one of illusion.

There are many tales about the perils of a mirage. A sunbaked traveler making their way across the endless stretches of a desert begins to fall victim to the oppressive heat and their thirst. Just as they doubt whether they can go any further, the traveler spies a shimmering image of shade-giving palms and a cool, bubbling spring-fed pool in the distance. They rush toward this paradise with all of their remaining strength—only to find that it's an illusion and that there's nothing there but more sand.

The lesson is that in our moments of desperation, we're all prone to see what we want to see—even if it's not really there.

The Material-Wealth Mindset is a mirage.

I was once convinced that, if I could accomplish the goals I'd set for myself, then everything else I might want in this world would just flow into my life.

But just as a few simple mistakes on the sea can send you dangerously off course, I didn't understand that a person's mindset can have a similar impact on their life. Living the Material-Wealth lifestyle was driving me further and further off course.

## Work, Work, and More Work

Work. Notwithstanding my mother's sage advice, that didn't just refer to what I did. It was also a fair description of who I thought I was at the time—or, at least, who I was trying to be.

If I managed to get any sleep, I'd wake up with a start very early the next morning. My day started even before my feet hit the ground, with my "monkey brain" firing frantically with emails and texts. Morning, noon, and night, I was in meetings and on calls, reviewing plans and contracts. I was making business connections, scouting building sites, and traveling from one corner of the world to another and back again.

I had a dizzying schedule that didn't leave much time for anything else.

My mother was right. I wasn't my business, but I was sure living like I was.

## Everything Has a Price

Life is equitable in the distribution of the most valuable asset: time. Every night at midnight, we all receive the same capital: twenty-four hours.

Rather than diversifying my investment of those assets wisely, I concentrated solely on my businesses. I was all in and doubled down.

However, life keeps an unforgiving account. With all of my time and energy invested in my businesses, I didn't have any personal capital left for family, friends, or taking care of myself. The toll on my health and relationships made me realize that not only was I spending every allotted twenty-four investment I received each day, but I was running up a debt on the other side too. I was sacrificing my present and compromising my future.

Everything has a price. When you're living the Material-Wealth Mindset, more often than not, it comes with an unmanageable personal cost.

## The Calendar Cage

Living with the Material-Wealth Mindset left me in what I call the "calendar cage." My schedule controlled everything. I couldn't spend time at family events or catch football matches with friends. I couldn't even decide when to sleep or eat. There were dozens of events on my calendar, and all of them were like the bars of a cage. It wasn't an issue of what I *wanted* to do; my calendar told me what I *had* to do.

Eventually, I wasn't serving my career. Instead, I was living in servitude.

Maybe you understand how dizzying a schedule can become and what that sort of confinement feels like. If that's the case, then I hope you understand the difference between service and servitude.

Service is a necessary component of a meaningful and flourishing life. It's based on a voluntary contribution of your time to benefit others, such as your community, family, business, and your true self. The important aspect here is that service is a completely voluntary action.

On the other hand, servitude is performing an act because you *have* to. There's no personal choice involved. When you're not free to make decisions for yourself, then it doesn't matter how well you're compensated. You're living a life of servitude, and ultimately, that means the rewards and returns for all of your effort won't be coming back to you.

## Joylessness

When I think back, what strikes me most profoundly is the overwhelming feeling of joylessness that characterized my time in servitude to the Material-Wealth Mindset. Those days didn't begin with an exercise of gratitude or positive visualizations. Instead, they started with a deep breath to brace myself for whatever storm I might be facing. Whatever free time I managed to steal away for family or friends was always shrouded by a dark cloud of guilt that I should've been working instead. On those occasions when I was able to feel a rush from achieving a goal or landing another deal, the thrill quickly subsided and was replaced by that all-too-familiar gnawing compulsion to move on to the next task.

This seemingly inescapable malaise was the first indication that there was something wrong in my life. I had an overabundance of drive but little passion. I had objectives, not dreams. I had everything I could want but little sense of satisfaction—and absolutely no joy.

My initial conclusion was that these feelings were the result of some defect within me, but after a good deal of introspection and a lot of self-work, I realized that these feelings were more a product of my situation than a personal reflection. There wasn't anything wrong with me, except that I'd been plugged into a system that had become obsolete over time.

Before we move along, I want to briefly cover the *how* of it all—that is, how we all came to acquire these mindsets in the first place.

Come along, I have someplace else to show you. It won't take long at all.

Take a look around. Do you recognize this place? They say that everything you knew as a child looks smaller when you return as an adult. This is your old school.

Does it remind you of more carefree times when you thought anything was possible?

I'm guessing you don't necessarily feel that way anymore.

I know that for me, somewhere along the way, I lost—for a time, at least—the wonder that had filled my childhood with infinite possibilities. It all started right here. Well, not your school but my school ... you get my point.

I went to school brimming with youthful enthusiasm, but what I learned was a system. My grades mattered more than what I actually learned. My performance was graded as a direct comparison with the rest of my class. One test led to another, and one grade level was followed by another. The ultimate objective was to position myself so that after graduation, I could take up the sort of profession that would allow me to provide the same education for my kids at the same school.

Sound familiar?

I'm in no way denigrating all of the wonderful teachers and administrators who dedicate themselves to educating our children—not at all. They provide an essential service to our society by growing, guiding, and strengthening our youth.

What I'm suggesting is that the underlying mindsets of this cultural routine are outdated. As I've said previously, I can appreciate the appropriateness—maybe even the need—of creating and perpetuating a system that's focused solely on generating external results, including riches and possessions. In the same way that humans instinctually follow each other, we also find great comfort in the status quo and are reluctant to embrace change. That's especially true when our patterns and routines are woven into the social fabric.

I understand this natural tendency to hold fast to traditional positions, but once I realized that my sense of discontent didn't originate from my shortcomings but from the obsolescence of our overarching systems, I faced the question of what I could change about it all.

I understand that there's nothing easy about change. Simply deciding that the old way doesn't work any longer and making the resolution to take a tentative step onto untested ground can be a challenge.

The inherent paradox in how those living with the Material-Wealth Mindset respond to change surprises me. The nature of business requires a person to analyze a system or product, identify what works and what doesn't, and then innovate the improvements that will make the business more efficient, successful, and profitable. Embracing change and thinking outside the box are necessary qualities for anyone who's going to achieve success in business.

So, why do so many high achievers who challenge the orthodoxy every day in their professional roles adhere blindly to an outdated system that's clearly failing to deliver on the promised satisfaction and fulfillment?

When I began to ask this question about myself and reconsider my outlook on my situation, I was initially intimidated by the thought of confronting practices that had been in play for generations.

It's ironic that what spurred me on in my personal quest were thoughts of my family legacy. When I began to blaze my path, I realized that when the Batterjees first imported Western medicines into Saudi Arabia, what they were also bringing along with them was dramatic change. Their courageous act to move into the future not only revolutionized healthcare in the kingdom and beyond but also played a significant role in opening the entire region to a wide array of beneficial new ideas.

I'm sure that many of your predecessors were mavericks—pioneers who weren't afraid to consider new ideas, embrace them, and put them into action. If you search your lineage, no doubt you'll find similar risk-takers and rule-breakers in your family tree. *Homo sapiens* might have survived through bonding, but the ones who won the evolutionary lottery were those who had the brains to think outside the box and the courage to take action.

We owe a great debt of gratitude to those who paved the way by embracing change. No doubt their sacrifices afforded us opportunities that were never available to them.

In that way, maybe changing some of the old ways isn't just our privilege but also our responsibility.

# CHAPTER SEVEN

## The Need for Change

Understandably, high achievers fear risking hard-earned success by deviating from the status quo. It's a phenomenon known as the sunk cost fallacy—when you're invested in a way of life, there's a natural tendency to cling to the familiar and a belief that recommitting and working harder will bring about more favorable results.

This sort of mindset keeps us stuck. The truth is that real change requires the courage to question assumptions, face fears, and take a leap of faith. That's not easy, but it's necessary for growth.

So, why don't high achievers apply that same business-honed, critical eye to reexamining the assumptions that seem to govern their life choices? What is it about change that holds them back from envisioning something better beyond the status quo?

Allow me to suggest that the answer can be found at the corner of Sixth Avenue and West 49th Street in Manhattan. Have a look around and take in the sights. We didn't come here to take in a show at Radio City Music Hall or see Rockefeller Center, though. No, I brought you here to introduce you to Manhattan's Diamond District. Within this couple of city blocks, there are more than 2,600 diamond dealers and jewelry shops. Almost every diamond sold in the United States passes through here. That's saying something when you consider that each year, diamond sales in America total more than $72 billion.[11] This is just one of the hubs of the international diamond market, which includes Dubai, Amsterdam, and Johannesburg—to name just a few locations. All of these markets account for global diamond sales somewhere in the neighborhood of $270 billion—around one trillion Saudi riyals.[12]

That's real wealth, right?

What would you think if I told you … maybe not?

Diamonds have been a prized commodity through the ages and around the globe. They've adorned the crowns of kings and queens, added sparkle to debutantes and actresses, and marked the engagement of millions and millions of couples.

But what exactly is the basis of a diamond's worth?

Your answer probably has something to do with the rarity of the stone or the nature of supply and demand in the marketplace.

Consider for a moment that modern technologies have opened the door to techniques that can create synthetic diamonds, which are made of carbon crystallized in an isotropic 3D form. Unlike previous attempts at manufacturing diamonds, these artificial products have

---

11 DiamondFacts.org, "The Diamond Industry Fact Sheet," accessed July 2024, https://www.diamondfacts.org/pdfs/media/media_resources/fact_sheets/Diamond_Industry_Fact_Sheet.pdf.

12 PR Newswire for Yahoo! Finance, "Global Diamond Jewelry Market Value to Surpass $265.29 Billion by 2030, Registering a Strong 5.19% CAGR, Driven by Increasing Disposable Incomes in Emerging Nations, Estimates Kings Research," February 6, 2024, https://finance.yahoo.com/news/global-diamond-jewelry-market-value-153000713.html.

the same chemical and natural properties as naturally occurring diamonds. When one of these man-made diamonds is placed side by side with one created by nature over eons, even the most experienced jewelers find it difficult to distinguish between the two.

If we're no longer dependent on the difficult and costly process of discovering underground deposits, mining rough diamonds, and then refining and cutting them to arrive at a final gemstone product, then this would seem to undermine the argument that a diamond's value is a reflection of its scarcity and associated production expenses. If commercial copies are more readily available, then how do diamonds retain their value and status?

I suggest that the answer is simply the reflection of a cognitive bias. That is, diamonds are valuable for no other reason than that a few people have told us they're valuable, and a large number of people believe that to be so. A diamond's value can no longer be based on its origin or the operations of a natural market—it is completely dependent on that shared belief.

In fact, the value of a diamond relies primarily on a narrative created by an advertisement.

The engagement ring dates back to the Roman Empire, when rings with a variety of gems were seen as an indicator of the groom's ownership. That custom continued until 1947, when De Beers Jewellers debuted their classic slogan, "A Diamond Is Forever," suggesting that the durability of the stone was representative of the proposed union. Two years later, "Diamonds Are a Girl's Best Friend" was featured in the Broadway smash *Gentlemen Prefer Blondes*, and Marilyn Monroe sang that tune in the movie version. The narrative was complete. From then on, every woman wanted a diamond in her engagement ring—the bigger, the better.

A diamond's value was no longer a matter of the stone's scarcity but of the narrative that convinced women that a key component of a lasting marriage was the rock in their ring.

Diamonds are by no means the only beneficiary of that sort of cognitive bias.

The perfect example can be found in the designer tags and brand logos that adorn so many of the products people admire and aspire to these days. Those marks don't have any function except to trigger our cognitive bias that the product has some increased intrinsic value.

I was on a casual outing with my extended family the other day. During our conversations with one another, a relative approached me, complimented me on my T-shirt, and asked what brand it was.

When I answered, they were surprised I wasn't wearing a more "exclusive" brand and suggested I ditch the no-name shirt—which they'd just admired—in favor of a luxury brand. When I asked if switching brands would give me a better shirt in terms of comfort, style, or performance, they were taken aback. In their way of thinking, the more expensive shirt was the better shirt because it was more expensive.

This relative is an exceptionally smart and savvy young individual, and it's because of their exceptional qualities that I included them as an example. If I'd presented a similar scenario in the guise of a business hypothetical, I'm confident they would have reasoned their way to the right conclusion that there'd be no sense in a business spending more when a reasonably similar product was available for much less. Outside the business world, in the context of their day-to-day life, this cognitive bias controls their decision-making without them being aware of it. Like so many others, they simply accept the narratives that others have established.

How about you? If I told you that a black T-shirt was 2,000 Saudi riyals and sold only in designer boutiques, while a blue T-shirt could be purchased for 40 Saudi riyals at local stores, which would you assume was the better T-shirt? Which would you want for yourself?

Maybe you think the answer is obvious.

But maybe, the only thing that's obvious in my question is how impactful and pervasive these cognitive biases have become.

Take for example the rise of internet influencers, an occupation to which a growing majority of young people currently aspire.[13] While there are countless benefits to be derived from living in the Information Age, there are just as many dangers inherent in this new way of living. I think that among these, one of the most insidious may be how social media has disseminated and perpetuated the Get-Rich Mindset around the world, particularly with the younger generations.

There are only a handful of social media sites, and this has funneled all of the users across the world into the same channels. The world was once a vibrant collage of different tastes and styles, but today, we see the forces of social media homogenizing people into copies of the same models. Where there were once distinctive regional cultures, today we find that the growing impact of social media is driving users to follow the same brands and adopt the same aspirations. More and more of those on social media—particularly the youngest and most impressionable—willfully surrender their individuality to follow the same trends. Besides wanting to wear the exact same clothes or listen to the same music, they embrace conformity and share the same limited outlooks and beliefs. That includes adopting the Get-Rich Mindset.

13 Recent studies have indicated that more than 80 percent of individuals between the ages of eighteen and thirty-eight have considered becoming a social media "influencer," and 25 percent have active plans on developing that as their career. Source: Morning Consult, "The Influencer Report," October 2019, https://pro.morningconsult.com/analyst-reports/influencer-report.

When I was a teenager and my parents' friends asked me about my future plans, I shared with them my dreams for an exciting career in business. Some of my friends talked about wanting to be doctors, architects, or engineers. Now, when I talk to adolescents—the future and promise of the world—the vast majority of them tell me about wanting to be influencers or brand models. In fact, recent surveys have shown that approximately 80 percent of Generation Z aspires to play these roles on social media, with one in four seeing it as their primary occupation in the future.[14]

Social media is controlling our collective narratives and unduly shaping people's decisions, making the most outrageous displays of affluence look like the norm. People are abandoning their individuality as they race after riches that, in many cases, don't really exist. These platforms are largely about deceiving their users with the illusion of wealth and fostering dreams of riches that aren't based on any meaningful reality. Unfortunately, they're also creating a controlling narrative.

I suppose that might be acceptable when we're talking about overpriced T-shirts or treating "likes" as if they're currency, but this mindset won't get a passing grade in business.

What I mean is that one of the primary functions of any business is to know the real-world value of materials bought and sold. When my companies are building hospitals or residential towers, we can't concern ourselves with what's fashionable. We need to access the highest quality materials at the lowest possible price to guarantee the standards of our product and the optimal return on our investment. That's absolutely fundamental to any successful business.

So, I'm always surprised when these principles being utilized every day by high achievers in business are abandoned when running their lives.

---

14 Morning Consult, "The Influencer Report."

It's no wonder that those with a Material-Wealth Mindset might prosper in business but fall behind in terms of the satisfaction they receive from their life experiences.

Among all of the concepts that have been worked into our subconscious as part of a larger cognitive bias, there may be nothing more debilitating than this shared definition of wealth as something that's primarily measured by the supporting narrative.

Let's take a look as to whether that's truth underlying all of this or whether your whole life plan might just be an overpriced T-shirt.

# CHAPTER EIGHT

## What's Your Real Value?

We've already discussed how most of us have been raised to think that wealth is measured by material success and how that system operates to our individual detriment. We've also covered the downside of the Material-Wealth Mindset and lifestyle.

What if I were to tell you that while you may have allowed this mindset to govern your life, that's not what you really want?

The average American will make about $2.7 million in their lifetime.[15] For the English, that's about £566,000.[16] In Germany, the figure is about €1,968,000.[17]

---

15 McLeod Brown and Chris Kolmar, "An Interactive Exploration of Dead End Careers," Zippia.com, July 10, 2018, https://www.zippia.com/research/dead-end-careers/.

16 Emily Cleary, "This Is How Much the Average Person in the UK Earns in Their Lifetime," April 25, 2022, https://uk.news.yahoo.com/average-person-uk-lifetime-earnings-143126977.html.

17 Bleona Restelica, "Working in Germany: Salary, Benefits, Days Off, & Everything Else You Might Want to Know," Schengen News, March 21, 2023, https://www.schengenvisainfo.com/news/working-in-germany-salary-benefits-days-off-everything-else-you-might-want-to-know/.

Obviously, that figure varies according to location, occupation, and several other factors. Still, because incomes and lifetimes are finite, there's a figure that represents the total amount that you'll earn. So, arrive at a figure of your choosing.

Got it? Now double it.

That's a lot of money, right? It's twice what you'll make in your entire lifetime.

Now, consider your potential work life—an average of about forty years, but life is finite too.

If someone offered it to you, would you sell those forty years of your life in exchange for the exorbitant amount you just calculated?

No matter how tempting that figure might be, the bargain would still be a losing proposition. This proves that, no matter how much you want wealth and position, you value your life more.

In the same way, dream up the ultimate dream house—perhaps on the beach or in a fashionable neighborhood. Would you move into this new residence if the cost was your health? Of course not. There's not a mansion in the world that's adequate compensation for something as precious as your health.

While the Material-Wealth Mindsetters may think they want all of the trappings of riches, maybe what they really want is something very different.

Not long ago, I was invited to an event that drew members of my industry from across the MENA world. The conference was held at Dubai's Atlantis The Royal, which bills itself as "the most ultra-luxury experiential resort in the world." It's a title that the exquisite property deserves.

The conference was capped off with an awards ceremony, and when my category was announced, I was humbled to be called out as the winner. As I made my way to the podium to deliver my thanks,

I was struck that the moment was the culmination of years of hard work by me and my teams.

If I still held the Material-Wealth Mindset, that might be the end of the story. I had a wonderful stay at a luxury resort, won an industry top prize, and positioned myself for bigger and better things to come. Period. On to the next goal.

However, that's exactly why so many people are dissatisfied with their situation in life. When you hold a Material-Wealth Mindset, those perfect nights come to an end, and you have to start all over again on your Sisyphean quest for more.

The next morning, I checked out of Atlantis The Royal, and those accommodations became just a memory. My prestigious award was placed on a shelf with the others I'd won over the course of my career. My usual daily workload had doubled because my attention had been diverted during the conference. There had been special moments, but I was right back at another workday.

As I've already told you, my story didn't end when I left Atlantis The Royal. In fact, it was only the beginning.

After my morning travel and a difficult workday, I was relieved to finally arrive home. My daughter is always happy to see me, but this evening, she greeted me with a special excitement.

She jumped into my arms. "Did you win your award, Baba?"

I'd told my daughter about the nomination when I left for the airport days earlier, but I was surprised that a girl so young would remember and mark its importance to me. "You remembered that?"

"Oh, Baba, I've been praying for the last three days you'd win your award," she beamed.

"Yes, baby," I said. "I did win the award."

She was so proud of me and her prayerful part in my victory that she threw her arms around my neck in a moment of pure joy.

And *that's* what really matters: joy.

That joyous moment will stay with me for the rest of my life. If it were possible to sell that memory, there isn't a monetary amount you could offer me in exchange for something that I value so much.

Some cynical people might roll their eyes and think that mentioning "joy" is being warm and fuzzy when I promised I wouldn't.

I'm always as good as my word, so just turn the page. I'll clarify everything.

# CHAPTER NINE

## The Joy Bull's-Eye

As human beings, we tend to accept as true, statements made by authority figures, whether there's any supporting proof or not. This effect is compounded when others in our social circle also capitulate. The more people believe the authoritative statement, the more deeply we believe.

We've discussed how the Material-Wealth Mindset is focused on wealth solely as a factor measured by material possessions and professional achievement. Because of this, we've been misled into thinking that our life's purpose is to earn, perform, and consume.

We've also discussed that, despite the professional heights someone might hit or whatever conspicuous consumption they might indulge in, there's nothing in the Material-Wealth Mindset that'll produce any lasting satisfaction.

Finally, I've suggested that maybe the reason for this pervasive lack of fulfillment, which exists even in those who seem to have it all, is that those material ambitions are based on the misguided notion that we want riches when deep inside, what we really want is something else: joy.

I have a passion for exotic automobiles, but I can tell you with authority that owning the sportscar of your dreams comes with the nightmare of storage fees and maintenance bills. The thrill doesn't come from owning the car but from getting out on the open road and appreciating all of the ways that automobile and man can be integrated into one incredible machine.

That's right. *Joy.*

It's not staying at a prestigious resort like The Atlantis that matters to me. Rather, it's my appreciation of its extraordinary aesthetics that brings me joy. The award I won is nothing more than a trophy made of wood and glass, but the recognition of my peers whom I deeply respect brings me joy. In addition, my daughter's reaction to that award fills me with joy.

That's the secret to this life: the most precious thing of all is joy.

What most of us are really seeking isn't money and things but joy.

Maybe some of you think I'm splitting hairs here, but you're mistaken. The distinctions I'm making might be subtle, but that doesn't diminish their importance.

That's why I've brought you here to this archery range. We're here because I can't think of a better place to talk about the importance of taking aim at the right target.

If you aren't familiar with the sport of archery, there are a number of different techniques, mostly separated by region. Arab archery, Chinese archery, and *kyūdō*—a Japanese martial art—are all examples, but there are dozens of styles. What they all have in common is that the goal of the sport is to hit a target with ten rings—two for each band of white, black, blue, red, and gold. Among these, the inner ten ring or bull's-eye is the ultimate objective.

I suppose you could say the difference (distance) between each of the rings on the target is subtle, especially at ninety meters, but those subtleties are what distinguish the winners from the losers in the sport. If for some reason you're not aiming for the right spot on the target, then you're more likely to end up as one of the latter.

Life is no different.

Those with the Material-Wealth Mindset take aim at material things, such as positions, acquisitions, and recognition, but the true bull's-eye they need to target is joy. The choices we make every day become the arrows we shoot. When we train them on maximizing joy rather than obtaining riches, that recalibration reorients everything in our lives.

I'd never suggest that business success or professional achievements aren't important. Nor would I try to convince you that luxury resorts and exotic automobiles aren't wonderful—I know differently. My message has never been about eschewing the material if you're interested in those things, as I am—very much. These items should be on your target in the archery match of life, but they're not the bull's-eye.

If you constantly take aim at the material items scattered around the outer rings of the target, you'll certainly hit the mark and score accordingly, but unless you're aiming for joy—the bull's-eye of life—you'll never achieve the highest score. True wealth isn't a measure of how much you own or what you do but of how much joy you have in your life.

Let's continue that proposition to its logical conclusion. If what we really want in life is joy and not possessions or positions, then it's only logical that wealth shouldn't be defined by material things but by the joy that fills our lives. Because of that, it's equally logical that our objective shouldn't be to get as much stuff as possible but to fill life with as much joy as we can.

On this basis, trading the Material-Wealth Mindset for one that's focused on maximizing joy is the most practical and productive step in terms of achieving real-world results that improve a person's life, including in the corporate boardroom.

I'm confident of this because I've seen this work.

When I began writing this, I shared my ideas with a friend in the United States. He was raised in a low-income home and became a lawyer as a pathway to the lucrative life he equated with happiness. After earning all the money he'd ever hoped for, he realized that what he'd built for himself wasn't a home but a house of cards.

During our initial exchange, he was polite but unimpressed. Two weeks later, however, he called me back. "I couldn't stop thinking about what you'd told me. It was hard at first, but the more I thought, the more I realized how misguided I'd been. Now that you've opened my mind to intentionally seeking joy, it's changed everything."

He's only one of many with whom I've shared this outlook and who have benefited as a result.

I'm not talking about passively waiting for joy to come to you. On the contrary, what I'm telling you is that you need to go out into the world and aggressively seek joy in every aspect of your life.

Turn the page, and I'll show you how.

# CHAPTER TEN

## Common Sense, Not Common Practice

I recently had the opportunity to attend a business conference held in a wonderful resort in the historic oasis town of Al-'Ula. One of the offered team-building activities was a morning hike in the surrounding mountains, and I jumped at the chance to go exploring.

A small group of us set off, but as is so often the case, our numbers shifted as the hike progressed. One of the members was older than the rest of us, and rather than leaving him to walk alone, I stayed back while the others raced ahead.

This elder gentleman and I talked casually about our respective businesses. Then, our conversation turned to my personal journey and my focus on maximizing the joy in my life. I shared with him some of my thoughts about redefining wealth.

He scoffed, "Everyone knows that. It's common sense." My new friend's reaction was neither unexpected nor unique.

I smiled. "Common sense isn't common practice."

"What do you mean?"

"You may be right that many people—maybe even most people—know in their hearts that living for money and things is folly, but that's certainly not how they live. And they may experience joy if it comes their way, but they certainly don't prioritize actively seeking joy in their life."

I continued, "Take this hike that we're on. Before the morning is over, we'll all end up back at the resort. When we do, all of us will have completed the same route and walked the same number of steps, but we won't have taken the same journey."

"What do you mean?" my friend asked.

"The others all raced forward with members of their groups. I was the only one who stayed back and took advantage of the opportunity to make such an interesting new friend."

I pointed to the amazing rock faces. "The wind has carved the sandstone into exquisite works of art, and the hills around us have supported human civilization since 5,000 BC, but the others are so fixed on tracking their workouts on their phones and taking selfies to post on Instagram that they might as well be walking on the treadmills in the resort's gym. So, we'll have covered the same distance, but I'm the one who'll come out wealthier for the journey."

My friend stopped in his tracks and looked at me. "Tell me more."

Nothing that I told my hiking companion or that I've written here is meant to express any sort of judgment about living life one way or another. On the contrary, while judgments and comparisons may be the chief components of the Material-Wealth Mindset, in order to achieve the Joy-Wealth Mindset, it's necessary to let go of all judgment and focus on your own state and story. I lived a large part of my life chasing purely material goals, and if that works for you, I wish you luck.

Some people come away thinking that I'm offering an easy way out. I think the misimpression exists because the Material-Wealth Mindset is often paired with endless working hours and checking boxes on lists. That's why some people think I'm somehow suggesting a less demanding approach to life, but this isn't the case.

In fact, I think the easiest path is to continue being a cog in the system, following the leader and accepting whatever life hands you.

By choosing to maximize joy in your life, you must abandon that comfortable system and forge a path of your own. You have to shoulder the responsibility for your choices, confront your fears, and push yourself beyond your accepted limits every single day. There's nothing easy about that.

To go one step further, maximizing joy requires making yourself present in every moment so that you can live with the fullest appreciation for all of the joy that life offers you in that experience. There's nothing easy about living so intentionally.

Please be aware that I'm not offering joy as a synonym for happiness. They're not the same. Joy is universally recognized as an extraordinary and extreme event and is necessarily temporary because of this.

Happiness is less well defined. The word has become overused and associated with a prevailing sentiment that everything can and should be pleasant all of the time. In fact, people have come to expect happiness to be the normal, constant state in life. If they're not perpetually in this state, they consider mere stillness as a symptom of some defect in themselves.

More than that, there's something passive about most people's concept of happiness, which they expect to come to them like a floating butterfly. Very few people *make* themselves happy.

In that way, happiness reflects an unrealistic expectation. I don't want to go too far down this particular rabbit hole, but some biological components of what we regard as happiness make it impossible—or, at least, unhealthy—to experience happiness as a prolonged state.

Joy, on the other hand, is something that everyone understands as extreme. Because of this, they're more receptive to searching and working for it in all aspects of life.

I'm not encouraging you to develop unrealistic or artificial positivity. This isn't about thinking that everything is rainbows and unicorns—just the opposite. The Joy-Wealth Mindset is about appreciating the strength of the storm you're facing and actively finding joy in the courage and skill you have to see your way through. These days, I anticipate that life will become difficult at times, but the joy I find in every moment is the force that keeps me buoyant through those rough seas.

Being your own sultan isn't about trying to achieve perfection. It's about finding joy in imperfection and refusing to be dominated by anything, including the natural tendency to surrender to life's difficulties.

The harder you look for joy, the more you'll find.

But first, there are some qualities you need to develop before you can be ready to maximize joy in your life.

# CHAPTER ELEVEN

## The Qualities of Joy

As with any development project, building a life that's focused on maximizing joy is a project of considerable scope, and there are more than a few preliminaries that are necessary for you to develop as well.

Before we move forward, keep in mind that transforming your life by seeking joy instead of riches is a journey that will continue for the rest of your life. This isn't a project with a completion date. Don't concern yourself with getting things done on a particular schedule. Spend some time sitting with your reaction to each experience and ponder your strengths and weaknesses and how you might develop them in the future.

### High Self-Worth

Perhaps more than any other quality, you must possess a high sense of self-worth. That is, in order to realize your dreams, you first have to believe in your heart that you're worthy of all you desire, including living a Joy-Wealth lifestyle.

A while ago, I was invited to attend an event in Riyadh at which Deepak Chopra was the lead speaker. After Dr. Chopra's speech, all of the event's guests were shown to a dining area, where a sumptuous buffet was laid out. As we queued up to move through the line, everyone excitedly talked about how engaging the night's speech had been and how much they all admired the man who'd delivered it.

However, I noticed that while everyone found a place to eat at one of the many tables around the room, Dr. Chopra was left alone at the head table. Although everyone admired him greatly, they were all too self-conscious and intimidated to request a seat at his table.

I marched directly to where he sat alone, introduced myself, and respectfully asked whether he'd like me to join him. He offered me a warm smile. "Of course."

We spent much of that evening in conversation, exploring our shared interests, particularly in personal self-improvement and developments in medicine. Our conversation was an invigorating exchange between equals, and I'm pleased to say that while I'd introduced myself as a stranger, we parted as friends.

I offer this story to support two rules by which I live my life.

The first of these is that when you see an opportunity, take maximum advantage. The evening offered me a chance to engage in conversation with one of the greatest minds of our time and provided me with an extraordinary educational opportunity that I couldn't have achieved in any other way.

The other and perhaps more important point is that while so many of my fellow attendees were unable to introduce themselves, I had a firm understanding of who I was and didn't hesitate to introduce myself. This is a reflection of my self-worth.

No one can ever reach beyond the ceiling set by their self-worth. In that way, everyone is effectively limited or empowered by their sense of worth.

If you don't think you deserve to have a conversation with Dr. Chopra, then you'll be unable to make that introduction. If you don't believe in your heart that you deserve to succeed in life, then you'll surely fall short of your aspirations. Most importantly, if you're not certain down to your very soul that you're worthy of a life of true wealth and joy, then the Joy-Wealth lifestyle will always elude your grasp.

This isn't arrogance or hubris. A positive sense of self-worth must always incorporate gratitude and reflect humility. This isn't about thinking you're better than someone else, because self-worth is knowing your own value and understanding you don't have to compare yourself to anybody else.

Living the Joy-Wealth lifestyle is dependent on clearing away the limiting beliefs that have been imposed on you and recognizing your limitless potential. You need to understand that life will never deliver what you think is beyond what you deserve. Therefore, you must build the courage to stand up for yourself and your interests.

You must regard yourself with the highest sense of self-worth. When this sense of self is combined with the certainty of *al sabr* (you'll hear more about this concept a little later on), a healthy physical state, and a champion's mindset, there's nothing that can prevent you from being your own sultan and taking up the challenge of laying claim to everything that's rightfully yours, including a life filled with maximum joy.

## Curiosity

The Material-Wealth Mindset strips away your natural curiosity. We're told that material wealth is key to life and our ultimate goal, and we never bother to consider the truth of that proposition or what other options may exist for us.

The important thing is to fully unleash that power.

The Material-Wealth Mindset is necessarily myopic. If you're only focused on material wealth, then your entire worldview is severely diminished. When I was focused almost exclusively on growing my businesses, my world was very small.

Once I opened the door to possibilities beyond the Material-Wealth Mindset, my worldview began to broaden. My mind opened to a wide array of interests. I traveled more and exposed myself to different people and cultures. My worldview expanded exponentially. This has become a part of my continuous pursuit of knowledge, which I know is a necessary part of achieving success.

This process of self-expansion not only made me wealthier as a person in the best sense, but it has also had the effect of making me a better CEO and businessman. When I'm confronted with the usual obstacles, I never flinch. Instead, I'm eager to seek out all possible solutions.

## Emotional Control/Emotional Intelligence

The Material-Wealth Mindset facilitates servitude by allowing other forces to control your thoughts and actions. By focusing on things, there's a tendency to overlook your emotions and the emotions of others.

When I talk about emotional control and intelligence, I mean two things: (1) understanding your own emotions and (2) how you interact with others.

There are real-world advantages to controlling your emotions and governing how you interact with others. Emotional awareness is necessary to maximize the level of joy in your life. Material-Wealth

Mindsetters see emotions as weaknesses, and they're often encouraged to suppress them. However, the psychological sciences have proven that our emotions are an early warning system. Ignoring our feelings is no different from turning a blind eye to a car's warning lights. Sooner or later, everything will break down.

For example, if you feel your stress level is too high, you should acknowledge this and take appropriate remedial measures (e.g., a moment of prayer or meditation or a walk outside) rather than allow the deteriorating situation to become an outburst in which you say or do something that will cost you over time.

These days, I recognize that an essential part of building my businesses is encouraging emotional growth in my teams at all levels. This is so clear to me now that I can't explain why I overlooked its importance for so long—and while other companies continue to do so. By developing a more positive work environment, I've created a more productive workplace. Encouraging and educating my team members have allowed them to bring more to the table in every facet of the game.

As a result of my efforts, my companies have consistently been recognized as some of the greatest places in which to work. Some with the Material-Wealth Mindset might dismiss these sorts of achievements, but I've learned that they're essential to success. Fostering my employees allows me to select the best candidates in their respective fields and keep them in my organizations over the long term. There's a real-world advantage to protecting and promoting our greatest assets: our people.

## Accountability

Accountability is closely related to emotional intelligence, but it deserves an independent discussion. One of the intoxicating aspects of the Material-Wealth Mindset is that many folks believe they carry with them a sort of immunity. That is, if they have certain assets or hold a particular position, then they can do no wrong and won't face any consequences for their actions. Unfortunately, many people take full advantage of this get-out-of-jail-free card in both their personal and professional lives.

Nevertheless, reckless behavior always eventually leads to disaster. The daily news is always filled with tragic stories of scandals and financial collapse, and I'm not sure whether that's karma at work or simply the inevitable results of human nature. In this technological age in which there are cameras everywhere recording everything we do, a single moment's indiscretion can have disastrous lifelong consequences.

One of the most important steps you must take to prioritize joy in your life is to adopt an absolute standard of accountability. As I like to say, "Nothing is your fault, but everything is your responsibility."

What I mean by this saying is that while my situation might not be my fault, it's still my responsibility. For example, it wasn't my fault that I found myself with a Material-Wealth Mindset, but it was my responsibility to take the steps necessary to find a pathway to a more meaningful life experience.

One of the first steps along that path for me was holding myself accountable for my actions, including my many missteps and mistakes.

Look, I'm not perfect, and I make any number of missteps every day. However, I've done a lot of self-work and found a mindset that I know has empowered me and others. I'm confident this can help you too.

The difference for me now is that I take ownership of my actions and don't try to avoid or deny mistakes. When you're free of that burden and focused on maximizing the joy in your life, every mistake is a learning opportunity and a chance to grow. Today, I'm only interested in ensuring that my mistakes don't reoccur and that I'm using every opportunity to the greatest advantage.

## Forgiveness

Closely related to accountability is the practice of forgiveness.

Despite our best intentions, every one of us makes mistakes and acts in ways that aren't in line with our aspirations for emotional intelligence. That's simply being human. To foster your personal growth and maximize the joy in your life, you have to be able to forgive yourself and others.

When I was stuck in my material mind, I was inclined to keep score of everything I did. Whenever I failed unrealistic expectations to always perform at the highest level, any perceived shortcoming was an open wound, and I would beat myself up until the next incident. At the time, I thought I simply had high standards, which would keep me disciplined and working hard. I see now that this cycle of self-abuse only inhibited me from opening up to my full potential.

You have to accept your failures and mistakes and cherish them as the learning opportunities that they really are to take the sort of action that any success requires.

As important as self-forgiveness is, the ability to forgive others may be even more essential. A cold fact of life is that people hurt one another. Sometimes, these slights are unintentional, and other times, the wounds are made purposefully. There's simply no way to walk this world unscathed.

This is why the spirit of forgiveness is so important. Arab culture offers a version of this maxim, but the insight that holding on to a wound and harboring a grudge is like drinking poison and expecting the offender to die is part of every culture.

Like everyone else, I've had my share of bumps and bruises. Do I set boundaries to ensure that I'm not disrespected? Absolutely. Do I maintain a strict admission policy for whom I allow into my circle? You bet I do. What I absolutely won't do is lessen the amount of joy I experience today because of something someone did to me yesterday. I forgive and move on.

From the very beginning, I've been conscious that there are readers who'll be cynically dismissive of what I share here because of their Material-Wealth Mindset. Still, I'm always amazed by how hardened businesspeople so often fail to manage themselves in a business-first manner.

I can't count the number of stories I've heard over the years of doing business in which someone was driven by some misguided act of vengeance, or passed on some potentially profitable business dealing, because of their wounded pride.

When you're focused on your own joy, you don't have time for those types of concerns.

Let it go, and let joy flow.

## Visualization

To access your fullest potential and maximize joy in your life, it's necessary to open your mind to embrace your creativity, which is the source of a significant superpower. While the Material-Wealth Mindset is based on blindly accepting the systems that are already in place and assuming roles within them, the Joy-Wealth Mindset understands that we have the ability to be the creators of our lives and destinies.

Throughout this book, I've described one scene or another and relied on your imagination to bring them to life as if they were movies. As we progress with building your new joy-centered life, that same ability will become vital.

First, building a new life is an act of creation. For you to discover what you really want out of life, you must work through several exercises using your imagination.

Second, I think very few exercises are more powerful than using your creativity to engage in meditative visualizations. This doesn't necessarily mean sitting on a yoga mat with your eyes closed. Rather, it's a deep thought process to include in every aspect of your life. When I develop a property, I mentally walk through every project detail from top to bottom, taking in every detail. This visualization is an extraordinarily helpful exercise.

To fully realize any dream, you must first envision every aspect. If you want to build a life based on joy, you must see that existence in your mind and walk through every aspect of that new existence.

Creativity is an essential element of your new tool kit for creating the Joy-Wealth Mindset. Now that I'm on my journey, I consistently apply these principles to every area of my life.

## Passion

The Material-Wealth Mindset is based on following established patterns to sleepwalk through life.

By contrast, the Joy-Wealth Mindset demands a true, fiery passion.

There's a significant difference between waking up thinking "Oh boy, I *get* to go to work today!" as opposed to the familiar "Oh man, I *have* to go to work today."

Everything in life improves when it's performed as a passionate act of love as opposed to a duty.

Of course, I still have difficult days in the office, but every obstacle I face is transformed when approached with passion. I absolutely love what I do every day, and that passion propels me through any obstacles I might confront.

## Persistence

Your biology and psychology are hardwired to maintain your current status quo, and the Material-Wealth Mindset is a part of that compliance. All of this makes personal improvement difficult to accomplish.

Developing the Joy-Wealth Mindset requires 100 percent commitment. Anything less won't get the job done.

In the same way, this transformative process takes time. You should expect a steep learning curve. So, if you're not committed to the journey, you won't get far.

Keep in mind that what we're doing here is talking about reorienting your entire state and creating a brand-new you. The result is worth it, but you shouldn't deceive yourself into thinking it's easy. You must completely dedicate yourself to your new joy-filled life.

## Confidence

While the road ahead is admittedly difficult, you must know before you take a single step that you have everything to make it through the journey and that you'll be successful in the end. Confidence is everything.

The Material-Wealth Mindset offers false confidence based on the bluster of possessions and positions. If these are lost, then confidence goes too. I've heard many stories of people who lived boldly when they had riches but who came completely apart when they suffered a reversal of fortune and had to face life on their own.

With the Joy-Wealth Mindset, confidence comes from the individual. When you're not concerned with external expectations, you're able to create real confidence by knowing that you can lose every possession and still get up the next morning with the determination to rebuild whatever you've lost. This is tied to Current Wealth. As the saying goes, "Let me fall if I must fall, as the one I am becoming will catch me."

## Purpose

The Material-Wealth Mindset derives its sense of purpose from blindly following the system of expectations. This lack of personal purpose is responsible for so much dissatisfaction. Ultimately, lack of purpose is the Material-Wealth Mindset's shortcoming because there's no real sense of purpose in those hollow pursuits.

Every human needs an independent reason to pursue their goals. So, in order to transform to a Joy-Wealth Mindset, you'll have to discover a purpose that's unique to you—something that gives real meaning to your life. You need to determine just what impact you want to have in life.

## Balance

One of the characteristics of the Material-Wealth Mindset is the tendency to take things to the extreme. You work too hard or spend too much. Everything is taken to excess.

Balance is power.

There are drawbacks to working all of the time, but a fierce work ethic is essential to the Joy-Wealth Mindset.

There's no lasting satisfaction in inconspicuous consumption, whereas there's great joy in having things you sincerely appreciate.

In the next chapter, you'll identify what you want to incorporate into your life, such as a family and a career. Balance is key.

## Gratitude

When I was a boy, technology was just bringing us the flat-screen TV. Those first units weren't a significant improvement on what we already had in our living rooms, but they were shiny and new.

One day after school, I approached my father with a deeply felt appeal about why our family needed to join this new trend in home entertainment. I think he might have been amused by my foolishness if he hadn't noticed that my request was tinged with envy.

Jealousy was something my father could not abide.

When I came home the next afternoon and went to the living room to watch my programs, the same relic of a TV was still there, but now it had a shiny, new feature: a sign that my dad had drawn up and taped to the bottom. The sign bore the following Arabic saying: "He who only watches others will die of worry." It was an admonition to always appreciate the blessings I'd been given in life without losing myself to jealousy or concern myself with what others had. What he was telling me and my siblings was that there would always be others who might have more than we do and that envy is a twisted emotion that shows a lack of gratitude and humility.

In the years since that afternoon, I've developed a mental practice to attach my father's sign to all of my many blessings. I consciously and intentionally express my overflowing gratitude.

From a practical perspective, I believe gratitude is an extremely important element in maximizing joy in my life.

The Material-Wealth Mindset operates on one single word: more. No matter what you achieve or what you buy, or have, there's a constant refrain of "more!" In many ways, a sense of gratitude is antithetical to that sort of lifestyle.

Gratitude—the realization that you have everything you need in the present moment—is the source of satisfaction. Within that, there's an opportunity to maximize the joy that you experience in your life.

After you've spent some time considering these qualities, it's time to move forward.

# CHAPTER TWELVE

## A Fresh Start

In my hometown of Jeddah, Saudi Arabia, there's no better place to take in all of the beauty of the wonderful city than atop one of my favorite development projects, The Vue. From this vantage point, we can see the waters of the Red Sea dancing to the horizon in one direction and the lights of the city sparkling like diamonds in the other.

I'm proud of the structure, and I'm equally enthusiastic about the role this project will play in the development of the surrounding neighborhoods and the Jeddah community. It's the realization of a dream that I've nurtured for a long, long time.

There are a hundred thousand complexities involved in building something of The Vue's size and magnitude. There are blueprints, engineering studies, and building plans for absolutely every aspect of development and construction. Everything must be thought through from start to finish, with no detail overlooked or left to chance.

This structure of steel and glass started as a dream of mine—a vision.

Building a life that's focused on maximizing joy rather than prioritizing material accumulation is no different. In the fullness of time, it will require you to make a plan and work it out step by step. Everything before that starts with a dream.

Before you can begin to live a life full of joy, you first need to find just what brings joy to your life.

That's why I brought you here to this room—well, again not so much a *where* as a *when*. And this day, well, it's your eighty-fifth birthday! Or, at least, you're going to imagine it is.

The human brain is remarkable, both in terms of what it can do and what it cannot do. Among its most significant limitations is the ability to distinguish between what is actually happening and what is happening within the mind.

Don't believe me? Take a minute now and think of the most loving memory you have; your mother singing you to sleep or a special moment with your partner or children. You'll immediately feel the warm flush of the same feelings you experienced in that moment as it actually happened. Now, think of a time when you were very angry or frightened and your body will tense to express your fury or face a threat that no longer exists.

And within this mental glitch is the power of visualization.

And I do mean *power*.

Now we're going to undertake a very transformative exercise that incorporates this incredible power to sort the confusing and possibly contradictory elements of your life that are preventing you from reaching true success. The goal is to envision your ideal life as a means of ordering and prioritizing all of the elements that are currently vying for your time and attention. Once you've gained a sense of the life you truly want, you'll be able to create an effective strategy for achieving everything that you want and everything that brings joy into your life.

We've previously discussed the limiting beliefs that the Get-Rich and Material-Wealth Mindsets create and the need to clear these toxic thoughts from your mind. This is a perfect opportunity to put that open mind to work by envisioning the perfect life that you'd lead if there were no limitations on your potential and you could achieve anything you worked hard enough to accomplish.

So, I want you to find a comfortable place where you can sit for a moment or two without any distractions or disturbances.

Close your eyes. Now, picture yourself as the guest of honor at your eighty-fifth birthday party after having lived the best life that you can imagine. This is the celebration of a life well lived—a life in which everything has turned out exactly as you dreamed it would.

As with any visualization exercise, one of the most important aspects is to immerse yourself in the sensory aspects of everything you imagine. What are the sounds and smells? How does it feel? The deeper you can fall into your vision and the more details you can generate, the better your results will be.

Where are you? Retired in a seaside villa or living in a country mansion or urban high-rise? How's your health on your big day? Are you able-bodied, or do you have physical limitations?

What have you done with your eighty-five years? What accomplishments are you most proud of? What was your career like? What were your biggest successes? What legacy did you leave behind?

Who's with you? Who do you see surrounding the elder version of yourself? Family? Friends? What are your relationships with these people like? What are your favorite memories together? What did you enjoy doing with them over the course of your life?

What are your hobbies? How do you spend your days? Are you still working or have you retired? What do you look forward to?

What are the things that brought you joy throughout your perfect life?

After you've completed the visualization portion of the exercise, I want you to write a description of your experience. Make a list of all of the items that matter to you.

You need to understand that you have total control over who you are when you reach your eighty-fifth birthday.

As a function of current and forecasted wealth, the investments you make in your future self will be realized in your forecasted wealth. If you assess your current wealth and make an investment in yourself today, then you can build whatever you want for your eighty-fifth birthday.

Your account of your ideal eighty-fifth birthday is a detailed version of your dream life. This is a road map for where you'd like to arrive in the future after living your life authentically and prioritizing bringing joy into your life. This will be a blueprint for building a life centered on the Joy-Wealth Mindset.

Now, it's simply a matter of setting a path to get you from here to there.

Bring your list, and I'll show you how to set a course.

# CHAPTER THIRTEEN

## Your Life List

For those who harbor the Get-Rich/Material-Wealth mentality, life goals and personal aspirations are one-size-fits-all. For those who aspire to a Joy-Wealth lifestyle, the list of elements that bring them joy throughout a well-lived life should be as individual as a snowflake.

With that in mind, I'll share the revelations that came to me when I walked through the eighty-fifth birthday exercise. I'm not offering this as any sort of template, but I'm here to give you some idea of the sort of considerations you might include in your list.

**Family** was the most important thing to me when I imagined myself at my eighty-fifth birthday bash. I wanted my wife by my side and to know that we'd shared a strong and loving bond. I wanted to be surrounded and loved by my children and to know that they were living fulfilling lives with children of their own. I wanted to be acknowledged as a wise and kind leader of this flourishing branch of the Batterjee family.

Beyond my immediate family, I wanted to be surrounded by my brothers and sisters and their children and my cousins and their children. It was important to me that there was a strong and loving bond between us all.

**Business** was next on my list. At my eighty-fifth celebration, I wanted to be known as a business leader who had made significant impacts on my own native Saudia Arabia, the MENA region, and the whole world. I wanted to have made this impact not only with my buildings but also with my innovative ideas and concepts. I wanted my company's IHCC to build impactful projects, Lifestyle Developers to have improved standards of living across the board, and for GREENER to have introduced new environmentally beneficial technologies. I wanted to be seen as a mentor who was directly and indirectly involved in the success of countless others. And maybe most important to me was that I wanted to have established a generational dynasty that would offer opportunities to my children, their children, and the Batterjees long after them.

**Financial security** was another consideration in this respect. I wasn't concerned about my accounts for their own sake, but I wanted to make sure that my family was well situated and would always be provided for. I wanted to have generational wealth that would always provide for my family, generation after generation.

**Community** also figured prominently for me. I wanted to be remembered by my community as someone who led by example in supporting my neighborhood, city, and nation. I wanted my altruistic and charitable works to have enriched the lives of many in the spirit of the old Greek proverb: "A society grows great when old men plant trees in whose shade they know they shall never sit."

**Friends** were another important element for me. At my imagined eighty-fifth birthday, I saw myself surrounded by all of my friends who had proven themselves over and over to me through the years.

I'm not talking about those who were along for the ride as long as the sailing was smooth, but about people who had proven they would stand by my side no matter what. Because of the distractions of the Material-Wealth Mindset, I wasn't always as attentive a friend as I should have been, but as with any true friendship, there was always a road back. Because I had made the necessary changes, these friendships were an essential part of my life.

**Self-improvement** was also a significant part of the picture. The journey of transformation had been an incredible adventure, and I was eager to follow wherever the path led. I had created new relationships and traveled the world as part of my efforts to expand my horizons and continue my commitment to education. I was also still keen to continue these efforts.

**Physical health** was the other element I prized. Not only had I planned on living a long, long time, but I also intended to make certain that I was vigorous over the entire span of my life. On my eighty-fifth birthday, I was determined to be the life of the party! I had learned the advantages of taking the necessary steps to ensure and improve my physical health, and I had always incorporated them into my life.

There. With one exercise of imagining my eighty-fifth birthday and the ideal life that would lead to such an event, I've managed to identify and isolate the elements in my life that provide me with joy: family, business, financial security, community, friends, personal development, and physical health.

Recall your experiences, take a look at your list, and maybe even rework it altogether. When you're ready and after you've had the opportunity to reflect on everything, put together a list of the elements in your perfect life that would maximize the joy you experience.

In the next chapter, we'll put together a strategy for implementing all of those elements into your daily life.

# CHAPTER FOURTEEN

## The Wealth Pie

It's Investing 101: diversification is key.

Markets and assets fluctuate, and diversifying insulates against these shifts. In simple terms, don't put all your eggs in one basket.

I'm always surprised that the Material-Wealth lifestyle creates a focus on only one aspect of life. When I lived to work and most of my focus was on business pursuits, I neglected other aspects of my life. As a result, when there were challenges in my professional life (all aspects of life ebb and flow, including careers), there wasn't anything in my life to offer the motivation or consolation that I needed in those dark times.

When things were difficult in the office, everything else seemed like more demands on me rather than what they really were: the answers to my prayers.

The more difficult those days in the office got for me, the more I followed the Material-Wealth Mindset by doubling down on my investment of time, energy, and attention in working even harder. If the workweek was particularly brutal, that was a reason to work harder over the weekend.

These days, when I think that something isn't working, the answer might be to find something that works better by using my creativity. But in those days, I was convinced that by working harder and harder within a system that I knew didn't work, I could somehow force a positive response. That was foolishness and another product of the Material-Wealth Mindset's propensity for creating false narratives.

Unsurprisingly, nothing about working harder made anything better. It took a toll on my relationships and ultimately began to have a detrimental effect on my health. This made me less efficient and productive in the workplace.

When I look back at my behavior, I see a familiar trend.

Anyone involved in stocks at any level has heard stories of investors who experienced terrible losses in the harshly fluctuating markets. Instead of cutting their losses, they only doubled down on their initial investments.

In all of those examples, we see the foolishness of focusing everything we have on just one thing. We fool ourselves into thinking there's some kind of virtue in putting more and more into a system that doesn't work and doesn't produce the promised results. We understand that's how investors end up bankrupt in business. In the real world, this is how so many people end up dissatisfied and unfulfilled—just as I did.

That's why I've brought you here. The wood-paneled offices, the top-flight furnishings—these could be the offices of any investment firm in the world, but this one is different. This adviser isn't here to manage your money and investments but to help you manage the assets that really matter.

Have a seat and take out your list of the elements in your life that provide you with joy—the ones that will matter to you when you're celebrating your triumphant eighty-fifth birthday. Those things are the assets that really matter, and if you manage them properly, they can provide consistent high-yield dividends of joy over and over again.

However, nothing works without a plan, so let's use my list as an example for you to create your investment plan.

I've already identified a number of assets that are essential in my life: family, business, financial security, community, friends, personal development, and health. These are all of the components that are essential to a joy-filled life for me. (Please keep in mind that this list will likely change as I do and will be adjusted accordingly. You should allow yourself the same amount of leeway with your list as you move forward.)

The Material-Wealth Mindset doesn't recognize so many important elements but focuses on just one or two—primarily business-related assets. As a result, the other assets are neglected. At the end of one's life, there's no chance to go back and revive those interests.

I wear several hats as the corporate leader of a number of businesses. I manage each one daily, devoting as much attention as they need at any particular time. If I were to devote all of my time to one company over the others, the favored business might flourish, but the others would suffer as a result of my neglect.

In the same way, if I were to strictly schedule the amount of time I spent with each company without any flexibility or variance, then I'd inevitably drop the ball with a company that needed extra time during a particular period and waste time with others that didn't need as much attention.

Remember that the key is to keep all things in balance and be flexible in all things, especially your utilization of current wealth and forecasted wealth.

Let's go back to the list I made during the eighty-fifth birthday exercise.

When I pictured my life on that momentous day, I realized that my family was the most important component—the one that filled me with joy most intensely and most often. To get to that point in my life many years from now, I need to develop my relationships accordingly. If I want my family to be around me on my eighty-fifth birthday, I need to be here for them now and in the future. I need to balance current wealth and forecasted wealth.

My businesses were also important to me. This means I need to assign a significant percentage of my time and energy to these pursuits with equal regularity.

The same process applies to all of the other elements that bring joy and meaning to my life. For everything I want to have on my eighty-fifth birthday, I must plant the seeds now and tend to them regularly throughout my life.

What I eventually ended up with was the Wealth Pie, a pie chart that represents the expenditures of my time and energy. The Wealth Pie is my version of the portfolio of investments that your wealth manager provides to you.

There are days when my family requires the majority of my time. Other times, I have to turn the majority of my attention to my businesses. For the most part, this is a rough representation of what my final Wealth Pie might look like.

# Wealth Pie

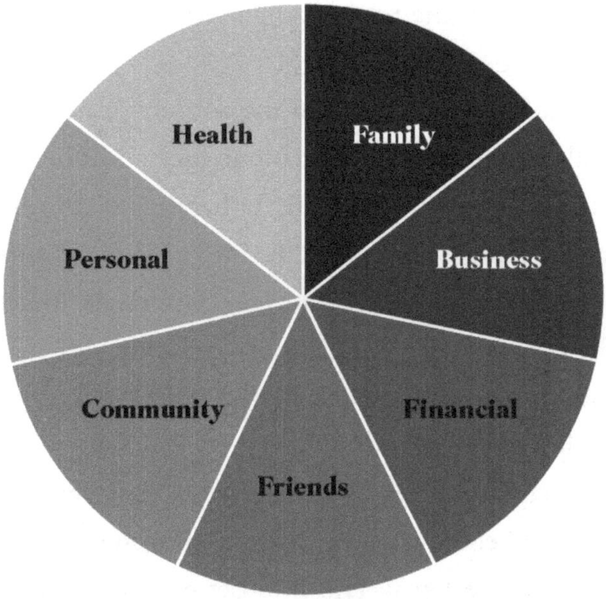


*Figure 14.1: My Wealth Pie. This is just a representation of the basic Wealth Pie; the amount of time and attention one devotes to each wedge will vary given specific circumstances.*

Just like the report I might receive from a financial planner describing my asset investment strategy, the Wealth Pie represents the distribution of my time and energy among all of the elements in my life that maximize joy for me. Individual days—maybe even weeks or quarters—will be different depending on specific circumstances, but the Wealth Pie adjusts for changing circumstances, just like fluctuating markets.

This system has a number of built-in benefits.

First, it ensures that everything that matters in my life gets regular attention. This prevents me from neglecting my family and friends or my personal development and health in pursuit of my business or some other item.

Second, it allows me to track the investments that I'm making in my ideal future.

Third, because I'm involved in the entirety of my life all of the time, it insulates me against the natural ebbs and flows of life. If I have a particularly tough day at work, rather than holding on to stress and frustration, I come home with the intention of swimming in the pool with my kids or watching a movie with my wife. That allows me to infuse my life with more joy. This, in turn, provides me with all of the motivation I need to head back to the office the next morning for another day in the business that I love.

It's essential to the Joy-Wealth lifestyle that you make investments of time and energy in all of these relationships, including your business. Because the Joy-Wealth mindset necessitates balance in all things, I offer one word of caution on how you invest your time.

In the same way that you can starve a relationship by not putting in the necessary effort, you can just as easily drown it by going overboard with too much time and attention. No matter the situation, whether family or business, when people get too much of you, you lose your value. Keep in mind our trip to the Diamond District and be mindful that it's the diamond's scarcity that keeps it from being just another rock in the ground.

Don't become too available or overaccommodating. When you give of yourself without restraint, the value and meaning of your contributions can be lost. As a result, the way that others view and appreciate you might become diminished.

You must always regard your time as the most valuable asset you have and spend it accordingly. Don't waste your time on unimportant things, such as pointless drama that's toxic in so many ways. Too much of anything is too much. You have to make your investments strategically so that you maximize your returns and no one comes to take you for granted.

The Wealth Pie is a basic guideline for creating a life that sustains the Joy-Wealth Mindset.

Now, it's time to get more specific.

# CHAPTER FIFTEEN

## Time Is Money ... and Life

Of all of the places that I've brought you to, this one is among my favorites.

This space with walls in gently soothing earth tones is open, wide, and welcoming. The tiled floor is always cool, and despite the abundance of windows, the midday sun never intrudes to make the room seem close or uncomfortable. There are an abundance of chairs and sofas, all of which are upholstered in soft, caramel-colored leather. The space is the perfect marriage of style and function because it was specifically designed to be so comfortable that all those who come to visit lose their sense of time.

The space is the waiting area of Sultan Batterjee Holding, where all of my offices are located.

As much as I love and am proud of this area, I try not to spend too much time there. I'm conscientious about making certain that no one else spends much time there either because if there's one thing I hate to see wasted, it's time.

Everyone's heard the adage, "Time is money." The implication is that time represents a portion of our potential to generate capital, but that's just another element of the outdated system in which our contributions or results are measured by the time that we expend. This sort of pervasive thinking doesn't reflect the standards of our new millennium, and it certainly isn't compatible with maximizing joy.

Time isn't a reflection of your opportunity to earn a riyal (or dollar or pound or whatever) but a reference to your life as a whole, including your opportunity to maximize joy. People aren't trading away their earning opportunities; they're selling off their life opportunities. Accordingly, when talking about wasting time, whether that's in a comfortable waiting room or in a professional position you've only taken for the money, what we're talking about is the most precious commodity you could possess: the opportunity to be your best self and fill your life with joy.

Unfortunately, part of the outdated system is a component that lies to us and fools us into believing that we have an abundance of time and that we can always put things off until tomorrow. Neither is true.

All you have is this present moment.

While many will blindly nod in agreement at that platitude, very few live in accordance with the underlying truth. Most people are content to trade their lives for a paycheck from an unfulfilling position because they somehow think they're getting the better of the deal by exchanging something that they have an endless supply of for that regular paycheck.

That's a fool's bargain.

If you're not getting the maximum return for your investment of time or if you're not seeing the joy in your life compounding regularly, then you've catastrophically mismanaged your time. You need to adjust your strategy immediately.

I'm imparting that sense of urgency not to be hyperbolic but because time is being wasted in two ways. The first is seen simply as the passage of days—the sort of wastage that many of us are familiar with.

The second is wasted time in the form of squandered opportunity potentials.

That is, not only are you wasting your time on the unrewarding exchange of a paycheck for a portion of your life, but the hours that you've fettered away could have been invested in a course of action that might have heightened your sense of fulfillment and expanded your joy. You haven't just wasted your time; you've also sacrificed everything productive you might otherwise have done.

Finally, I've observed that while I'm determined not to waste one second, too many people spend their entire lives in a waiting room of their own construction. Instead of taking action to improve their lives, they're content to sit back and allow the days to pass them by while they fantasize about what they're going to do tomorrow. Perhaps that's the most tragic waste of time of all.

There's no need to act impetuously in anything, and every endeavor requires preparation, but few habits are more toxic than the "tomorrow outlook." Every day gives you an opportunity to take action. Whether it's launching a new business or setting out on a new life course, there's certainly every opportunity to do *something*.

Read about and study the field you want to enter. Dedicate yourself to something that's going to strengthen your body or educate your mind. There are opportunities everywhere around you to take immediate action. Everything else is just an excuse to continue wasting time and wasting your life.

One last word on this subject before we turn to other topics: if you're consistent with all of these little efforts, they will compile and compound to produce big results.

There are myriad studies that have established that you only need to spend about one hundred hours to master most skills or achieve expertise in most subjects. Broken down over a year, this means that if you devote just eighteen minutes of your day to whatever you want to master, such as playing a musical instrument, learning a foreign language, or exploring technological advancements in your industry, you'll have spent one hundred hours in that pursuit at the end of a year, and you should be among the top 10 percent in that space.[18]

There's an old saying: "You can't cut the mustard if you keep cutting corners." This means that you have to do everything the right way because how you do one thing is how you do everything. When I point out the possible yields you can reasonably expect from devoting eighteen minutes per day, I mean actually making a concerted effort to master the material. Too many people think that there are rewards to be reaped from simply checking boxes and watching the hands on their watches, but that's not the case.

Do the work, and don't just go through the motions. You need to invest every moment with your maximum possible intensity. If you do that, then the rewards will take care of themselves. Spend your time wisely and with true dedication to achieving the goals you've set for yourself.

---

18 Gaurav Dayiya, "How to Reach the Top 1% by Using the Modified Rule of 100: Use the Magic to Upgrade Your Life," Medium, November 3, 2023, https://medium.com/practice-in-public/how-to-reach-the-top-1-by-using-the-modified-rule-of-100-cb6d21e7e9a1.

# CHAPTER SIXTEEN

## The Essence of Sabr, Realistic Expectations, and the Power of Consistency

There are many philosophical concepts that are unique to the Arabian culture, but one of my favorites is the principle of *al sabr*.

Some might translate sabr as "patience," but that falls short. In the West, patience often means merely controlling impatience, leashing expectations while watching the clock. Sabr is much more refined.

To begin with, sabr is a more evolved form of patience—one blended with the courageous acceptance of what will be. I don't mean that in the Western sense of que será, será (what will be, will be). It's more in line with the classic concept of *amor fati* (love one's fate) or accepting and loving your fate. There's more involved than a stoic's blind acceptance. Sabr is about having the courage to face your future and the faith to do so with the absolute certainty that everything will be as it should be or, to put it another way, that everything will work out in the end.

This combination of courage and faith is essential to make the necessary changes in your life.

You must possess absolute certainty that this isn't going to be something that you're going to try but a transformation that you're determined to accomplish.

One of the most discouraging experiences that I've had whenever I speak with people about reworking their lives by redefining their concepts of wealth is hearing them frame their intent as "I hope I can do this" or "I'll try to do that" rather than in terms of optimism for creating an improved lifestyle.

"Hope" is troublesome because it suggests that there's something other than your initiative that's ultimately responsible for the results you achieve in your life. Hope is a passive state that puts you in the position of waiting for some factor you don't control, such as fate and happenchance, to determine the conditions under which you'll live your life.

Similarly, "try" opens the door to the prospect of failure before you've even begun. If you haven't even started and you're already considering failure scenarios, then your objective is already tainted.

"Try" also suggests that you're not willing to fully commit; you're only willing to try. Such a half-hearted effort will never bring your vision to complete fulfillment.

The plan that I'm proposing to intentionally bring joy into your life requires absolute personal commitment, so there's no trying involved. This has to be something that you're going to achieve, no matter what it takes to make it happen. Because of that, hope isn't a factor because, from the very first start, you're absolutely certain that you're going to accomplish your goals. That iron-clad determination is necessary. Certainty is the mother of all skills.

Keep in mind that this doesn't mean that your forward progress will be easy or without obstacles. You may even feel as if you're sliding backward from time to time. Challenges should be expected and factored into any plan, as should the only reasonable option for handling them: working straight through them.

Because you should anticipate encountering difficulties in this journey, you should also establish reasonable expectations from the very start. What we're talking about here is rethinking concepts that not only have been instilled in you from your earliest beginnings but have also been an integral part of nearly every aspect of society for as long as you can remember. These are well-established and deeply ingrained traditions, which simply won't be addressed and reworked in short order.

For that reason, I don't think that I can overstate the importance of setting reasonable expectations for yourself in this and all your future undertakings. It's self-defeating to create unrealistic expectations that guarantee failure and, ultimately, surrender.

Those who decide they're going to lose an unhealthy amount of weight with an unsustainable diet plan or who set their sights on beginning an exercise program with an extreme regimen of running or lifting weights will not only fail miserably in achieving their goals, but they'll also inevitably use those personal shortfalls as reasons to quit and justification to avoid any future attempts at self-improvement. Crawl. Walk. Run.

Even worse, these types of experiences contribute to the limiting beliefs that many of us have developed over the course of our years in a system that prioritizes monetary acquisition as the only metric of success. To protect ourselves from the pain of these losses or the shame of our perceived shortcomings, we're too eager to underestimate our true potential and capabilities and settle for outcomes that fall far short of what would otherwise be possible for us.

There are many causes and explanations for these subconscious landmines—far too many to discuss here. The important takeaway at this juncture is to understand that while you might be consciously intent on achieving success, for far too many of us, there is an assortment of unseen psychological saboteurs that are lying in wait to destroy your best efforts to realize your ideal future.

In all too many instances, the biggest obstacle standing between you and the success you desire and deserve is you.

So, what to do?

This may seem like a complicated situation, and I suppose on a psychological plane, there are many nuances to consider. But as a businessman and developer, I don't look at problems; I find solutions.

While there are certainly no one-size-fits-all fixes, I've discovered that there's a basic practice for effectively dealing with this conundrum and positioning yourself to reach your goals that would otherwise be frustrated by deep-seated booby traps.

Because these limiting beliefs and acts of self-sabotage are primarily located beneath the surface in the depths of your subconscious, you need to develop your solution and work your plan with conscious intention.

As a first step, you've got to establish what you want to achieve. For right now, outlining your dreams will suffice. Be aware that this is the first encounter you're likely to have with your internal demons. These limiting beliefs will tie you down with considerations of what's reasonable or practical. All of that's nonsense.

In fact, since we've already acknowledged that there will be obstacles and shortfalls in your future, you might as well create dreams that are far greater than anything you think is possible for you to achieve in this life. In other words, as my father has always told me, if you want to reach the moon, you need to shoot for the stars.

My rule of thumb here is that if your dreams don't scare you, they're too small.

Once you've set your "impossible dream," the next step is to calculate a functional plan for reaching that height. Don't use this as an excuse to scale back your dream. Instead, figure out the path to reach your destination.

Then, as we've discussed, break that path down into steps and commit yourself to moving forward no matter what obstacles you encounter. Setting this mindset of moving forward toward your wildest dreams no matter what is the essential step in the process. This will keep you moving forward and lessen your discouragement and suffering when your way forward becomes difficult. Each setback will take an emotional toll, and indecision will be the source of your struggles.

For those who've made up their minds with unwavering certainty, there's no frustration to be found in the obstacles they encounter—just a need to dig deeper into their well of resolve and find a solution to what they know is just a temporary distraction from achieving their goals. This is the power of visualization.

To facilitate developing this necessary mindset, the best strategy is to develop a strict schedule that accommodates your goals and follow it absolutely. For example, if your health goals are to obtain a heightened level of physical fitness, then setting a daily time when you go to the gym to work out and following that routine will preemptively defeat the subconscious saboteurs that might tempt you from the path with thoughts of staying in bed for an extra hour's sleep.

In the same way, if you're committed to having a family dinner every week or a date night with your significant other, you'll find that the commitment you've made with conscious intention will deter the personal saboteurs that will pop up and try to dissuade you from the path that you've chosen for yourself.

At the same time, you should understand that no matter how set you are in your commitment, there will inevitably be occasions in which you fall short and turn over in bed instead of heading to the gym or find yourself unable to cancel a vital work assignment instead of following through with a scheduled date night. Things happen. The key here is not to react but to simply redirect.

One of the reasons for setting realistic expectations for your efforts is that this prevents you from letting your response become unreasonable. A skipped gym session or a missed date night isn't an excuse to abandon your discipline altogether or quit outright. Instead, you need to understand that no one's perfect and that situations are beyond your control sometimes. That's not a reason to mentally punish yourself or give up altogether. In fact, you may find that a gym-free day is sometimes beneficial, and an emergency night spent working instead of at the movies with your significant other can be necessary.

As soon as you can, return to the schedule you set for yourself with active intention and continue as if there hadn't been any disruption to your routine at all. The most important factor isn't perfection—it's consistency.

Results don't happen overnight. They happen over time. If you remain consistent, work hard, and stay patient (sabr), you can achieve anything to which you put your mind.

# CHAPTER SEVENTEEN

## No Such Thing as Problems

I try to focus on the positives, but before we continue with our discussion of how to put together specific pieces of your personal Wealth Pie, let's take a brief detour to the negative side of things. Let's consider some of the things that you should never do.

We've already discussed the emotional power that words contain and the real effects that they create. Because of my understanding of how a single word choice can change everything, I'm very careful about my use of language. I caution you to do the same.

While I'm extremely selective about the words I use, there's one that I not only refuse to use personally but also prohibit anyone in my teams from using. The word is "problem." I never use this word and hate to hear it from others.

There are a number of reasons for my hard deletion of this word. The first is that it contains so much emotional power. It's an alarm bell that inspires panic and brings out the worst in people.

Too many people associate a problem with an assignment of blame and respond by focusing on insulating themselves from culpability by offering pointless explanations and/or directing blame elsewhere. The use of "problem" typically precedes an emotional event that's never helpful.

"Problem" also suggests that there are unavoidable negative consequences arising out of the situation. As a result, people tend to fall into the fawn response, passively accepting that something has gone wrong. They greet problems with their hands in the air, as if there's nothing that can be done but accept whatever fallout might come their way.

Instead of entertaining all of the emotional baggage that accompanies a problem, I intentionally think of unintended situations as obstacles or challenges. Both of these words place importance on finding solutions and minimizing the potential fallout. No one worries about blame for an obstacle, and their response to a challenge is to find a resolution. In every aspect of my life, including my business affairs and personal matters, my focus is solely on maximizing results.

While we're on the subject of actions that interfere with realizing a life based on true wealth, there are several other counterproductive practices that you should put an end to immediately.

I consider almost all of what I've offered here on these pages to be advice. You're free to consider and implement it in your life or dismiss it out of hand as you see fit. Everything I've set out here is based on my experience and research. While I stand behind everything, I'm not asserting myself as an expert or a guru. I'm just a fellow life traveler like you. I've put my philosophy out there for you to decide whether there's value in it to incorporate into your life.

But if there's one exception to this, one instance in which I'll offer you an absolute, it's this: Never complain. Never. Not ever.

I'm not at all suggesting that you won't have reason to complain. Like the rest of us, no doubt you'll have ample reason to give in to the temptation to share with someone else just how rotten the world is or how badly a person has treated you. No matter how richly you deserve the right to express your dissatisfaction with life, nothing good will come from sharing it with someone else.

First and foremost, as far as I'm concerned, complaining lets the world know that when you're confronted with a disadvantageous situation, your first reaction isn't to find a solution but to give in to your frustrations and emotions. No matter how understandable that may be in the situational context, that's the mark of a weak will and an even weaker mind. Complaining demonstrates a victim mentality, and while some may feel empathy or pity for you and your situation, a person of character won't respect this.

The victim mindset manifests in those who won't take responsibility for themselves. Instead, they blame everyone and everything else for their failure to take control of their lives. These people have already admitted defeat in life and surrendered. Unfortunately, there's not much joy for someone who's ceded control of their life and given up on themselves.

Second, complaining is usually accompanied by blaming someone else for what's gone wrong. This shifting of blame also tells the world that you're unwilling to accept responsibility for your situation, even if it's unfair.

Third, complaining is also a tell that you're passive and willing to let others control you and your fate. Even when someone acts maliciously toward you, it's essential to demonstrate an assertive disposition that showcases your can-do attitude and denies others the power to exert that sort of influence over you and your circumstances.

Furthermore, complaining can have an effect on the people with whom you share your troubles. Every one of us has reason to complain, but strong-minded individuals will resent that you sought to share your burden with them. You'll only succeed in alienating the individuals you should be cultivating as allies.

Finally, your complaints are likely to draw other complainers to you. As the saying goes, "Misery loves company." Before long, you'll be surrounded by people who are looking to dump their troubles on you. These aren't people who can offer you inspiration or suggest solutions to your challenges. Because we're all shaped by the people whose company we keep to some extent, this circle of complainers can only pull you into a downward spiral of negativity. You become like those with whom you surround yourself.

While I'm addressing the subject, don't just refrain from complaining about your circumstances. Don't criticize anyone else's either. People use criticism of others as a way to divert attention from their issues and shortcomings. If you're paying attention to your own life and your own course of action, there's no need to offer a commentary about anyone else.

Anyone wise enough to understand how life works will know that if you're criticizing someone else behind their back, you're likely criticizing the person you're talking to behind *their* back too. Because of that, criticizing others will ultimately accomplish nothing, and it will undermine the trust that others have in you.

Don't complain. Don't criticize. Ever.

It's important to eschew these mental weaknesses for a positive mindset—a champion's mindset.

Extraordinary people and athletes are everywhere, but champions are rare. I had the opportunity to teach one of my sons this recently. He was working on a lengthy project with me, and at the last stage of the process, he turned to me and said, "I'm done. I want to do something else."

I told him, "That's the difference between a winner and a champion. A lot of people work their way through the process and devote tremendous effort along the way, but at the very last stage, they pull up short and quit. But that moment is when the magic happens. That extra push, that special stamina turns winners into champions."

I assured my son that I understood he'd already spent an extraordinary amount of time and attention on our project, especially for someone so young. I recognize that for all of us, the moment when so many want to quit is marked by soul-crushing fatigue, heart-breaking despair, and the fear that we've reached the end of the line and exhausted all of our personal resources.

All of the time, I see people in the business world devote themselves to a project and dedicate an extraordinary investment of time and energy to it only to come up short just as the deal should be crossing the finish line.

This is where the concept of al sabr comes in. You must have the patience, strength, and faith to endure whatever obstacles come your way, including your weariness. You have to make a commitment in your heart that you will never quit and that you will continue on your path until you reach your goal. No exceptions, no excuses.

That's what makes the difference between winners and champions. Lots of people may win lots of games, but very few people become true champions.

I've always been an enthusiastic football fan. I recently had the pleasure of attending the Champions League semifinals in Madrid to see Real Madrid CF take on FC Bayern Munich. (More on that monumental trip and the friends who shared it with me when the subject of this book turns to friends.) Anyone who shares my enthusiasm for football, whether they're a Real Madrid supporter or not, understands that there's something special about this team and the whole organization—something that makes them champions.

This particular match was phenomenal. It was exciting and hard-fought from the opening kickoff. However, as the final minutes approached, Real Madrid trailed by a goal. With every player on the field pushed to the point of exhaustion, there was little hope that they could overcome that deficit. Most teams couldn't have.

With less than two minutes left, Real Madrid scored a goal. With extra time put on the clock, Real Madrid did what everyone at the Santiago Bernabéu Stadium had previously thought impossible: they scored the winning goal and took the match. They'd made two goals in under eight minutes. They scored when it mattered most—when there was no other option but losing and failure was not an option.

After the game, when we reviewed the miracle we'd witnessed with other fans and analysts, everyone said that this was a classic move for Real Madrid. They always win in the last ten minutes because whether or not they bring the most talented team out onto the pitch, they always bring the team that's going to play their hardest without ever letting up from the opening to the closing whistle.

Unsurprisingly, Real Madrid went on the European Cup/UFEA Championship League for the fifteenth time in their history—more than twice as many times as any other club in the league.

On the whole, the difference between a winner and a champion is vastly underestimated. A champion keeps pushing to the point when everyone else tells themselves they want to rest or need to quit, and then they push themselves even harder. How they feel or whether they're motivated doesn't matter. A champion finds a way to keep going when everything else has turned against them. None of us can control what life brings our way, and to reach that level of excellence, we have to make a commitment to ourselves that we won't stop until we reach our goals. Most average people are quick to reassure themselves that champions have special talents or heightened abilities that the rest of the world lacks, but the truth is that the only thing that separates champions from everyone else is that they have the will to overcome anything—even themselves. This makes all of the difference in the world.

# CHAPTER EIGHTEEN

# Building Your Wealth Pie

With your personal goals identified and your mindset committed to building a life in pursuit of true wealth, let's assemble your Wealth Pie. Because you'll be investing all of your time and energy—everything you are—I'd like to take a moment to offer you the same sort of advisements that would preface a traditional financial investment.

## Be a Smart Investor

What I'm offering is a personal investment plan that has proven transformative for me. However, your results will depend on your level of dedication in following the process.

First, verify the plan for yourself. I've shared my philosophies with you, but I'm not didactic about this. You should consider what resonates with you and what you want to do with your life. Whether you have the courage or clarity of mind to follow it, I believe that deep down, you know your own truth. Always do what's best for you.

Second, even the best investment plans demand constant diligence. You can't expect to make an initial investment and then just walk away without tending it regularly. You need to keep a constant watch on where you've made your investment and vigilantly take the market's pulse. This scenario requires as much diligence. To fill your life with joy, you can't simply make a list and walk away, thinking that everything will take care of itself. This is a plan that you'll need to work on every day, 24/7/365. To be effective, it must become your new way of life.

Third, there's always an element of risk involved in any investment. Even the most reliable blue-chip stocks carry some degree of a gamble. There's no such thing as a sure thing when you're investing your money, and there certainly isn't one when you're investing your time and energy either.

This is particularly true when you consider that much of what offers us true wealth and brings us happiness and satisfaction in life are the human relationships that we incorporate into our own experiences. What I'm saying is that, in a very real way, investing in your own life requires taking a gamble on investing in others who are outside your control.

People change, and because of that, there's an uneasy but unavoidable balance that needs to be struck.

Building relationships with others who bring true value to your life experiences can pay the greatest dividends. At the same time, investing in someone who doesn't justify that personal commitment can have the same detrimental impact on your personal situation that an underperforming asset can have on your finances—maybe worse.

Most investors who have experienced some turbulence in one market or another are well positioned to make a rebound, even if the losses suffered do sting for a while. On the personal side of the equation, however, these types of loss scenarios can be devastating. Investing in a friend who turns their back on you or making a commitment to someone as a spouse or significant other who then betrays you can create situations that can reverberate with negative ramifications for years—if not decades.

You need to be constantly vigilant and regularly reevaluate your position. What might have been a good investment last month could sour because of deteriorating circumstances. You need to stay on top of all of your investments, be brutally honest with yourself about their performance and prospects, and be ready to make any necessary adjustments. Perhaps someone important enough to you that they deserved to be a wedge in your Wealth Pie has demonstrated that they're a losing proposition, or maybe you've met someone new who deserves to be brought into your Wealth Pie. You need to adjust accordingly.

In other words, your Wealth Pie is a reflection of you, living and constantly evolving.

You must attend to it every day if you want to receive dividends in the future.

## There's a Cost to Everything

One last point about investing in your financial portfolio or your life: there are always risks and reciprocal costs.

If you buy stocks in Company X, there's always a chance that the stock will tank. There's an opportunity cost as well, as your investment is money that you can't put into Company Y or Company Z, which might outperform your selection.

The same is true for the investments that you make in your life. There's a cost for every decision you make.

In terms of pursuing a life based on true wealth, I'm reminded that I recently spent a week in Australia at an Entrepreneurs' Organization seminar. I was returning to the airport when I struck up a conversation with my rideshare driver. We soon found ourselves discussing many of the subjects I've raised in this book.

He took immediately to the ideas I expressed and was kind enough to share this story.

He'd once been a manager at an upscale restaurant in Sydney—a very high-pressure position. His days were filled with administrative duties, and his nights were consumed with the operations of the place. He told me that he worked all of the time, and I told him that I understood.

He said the demands of his restaurant job took a toll on his family and prevented him from being as involved as he wanted to be, but he thought it was better to continue providing all of the material extras to which they'd become accustomed. So, he kept working and working and working.

That is until one day, he was getting ready for the night's service when he got a call from his teenage son from whom he'd become somewhat estranged because he was constantly occupied with work. His son was calling to ask if he'd be attending a school event in which the boy was participating. My driver said that he had a busy night ahead, but he could tell from his son's voice that if he added this event to the long list of skipped events, he was likely to lose his son forever.

There was no one to cover for the man, but he was convinced that his relationship with his son was on the line. So, he left the restaurant just as the dining hours were about to begin and raced off to his son's school.

Because he simply walked off his shift at the restaurant, the man lost his job and perhaps any opportunities to find a comparable position. Remember, I met him as a rideshare driver.

When I asked him about the price he'd paid for making that decision to abandon his post and rush off to his son's show, the man told me that the way his son smiled at him when he looked out into the audience and, to his surprise, saw his father was worth all of the consequences.

Everything has a price.

What was the price that my Aussie friend paid? Was losing his job because he chose to go see his son the price he paid? Or was it the time he missed with his son because he was committed to his career?

I don't know what the right decision was in this instance. I suppose only my rideshare-driving friend can answer that. I'm merely making clear that everything has a price and that the journey of redefining wealth to maximize joy in your life is no exception. The decisions and investments you make all come with a price, so make sure you weigh the costs and invest wisely.

Life isn't always as orderly as your Wealth Pie. There'll inevitably be occasions when circumstances dictate that you have to devote more time and energy to one wedge of the pie at the exclusion of some others. Sometimes, you need to focus on business until you get some pressing project completed, while other times, you're off with your family on vacation and focused entirely on them. Even within a single wedge, you may need to allocate your personal resources. Sometimes, my oldest child needs extra guidance from me, while other times, my youngest needs guidance or my middle child needs reassurance. Life is a balancing act, and maintaining your Wealth Pie will certainly reflect that.

One of my strategies is what I call "chunk time." When I know I have a big deal on the board, I'll give my business a block of focused time and energy, knowing that this will limit my time with family and friends. When the work is done, I immediately rectify that imbalance by devoting a block of time to my family and another to my friends. Through this balancing act, I am able to ensure that over any extended period, I remain true to the values at the heart of my Wealth Pie (current wealth) and make an investment to produce the long-term results that I want in my life (forecasted wealth.) It's about making the most of every opportunity in the present moment while strategizing to reach all of the goals I've set for myself on my eighty-fifth birthday. Everybody gets what they need, including me.

I recently took a brief vacation with my family at our beach house on the Red Sea. My children were all excited about the adventure, and one of my sisters brought her children along too.

The weather was perfect for taking the boat out onto the blue water and speeding across its wake on Jet Skis. This exhilarating experience was incredibly liberating and conjured up a thousand memories of similar wonderful afternoons I'd spent with my family in my youth. As I pulled off all of the spins and jumps that I'd learned on a Jet Ski so many seasons ago, I felt like a kid all over again.

"Baba, how are you doing that?" my children asked, their eyes wide with admiration. Although I've won a few industry awards, being the coolest guy on the water in my children's eyes might be the greatest honor I've ever received. "Can you teach me how to do those moves, Baba? Can you teach me?"

As I shared all of the tricks I'd learned when I was a child with my children, I felt like we were able to connect not only as father to child but also as kid to kid. The moment was magical, and our respective roles and age differences disappeared. We were all just guys reveling in the excitement of being together out on the water.

I was overwhelmed by an indescribable sense of joy in being connected with my past, present, and future. Not only was I reliving my youth and spending a magical moment with my children, but I was also aware that I was passing on a tradition that my children would someday share with their children—and they with theirs.

While such moments were spontaneous, the event was very much part of my strategic plans for creating current wealth (i.e., enjoying the water with my sons) and forecasted wealth (i.e., establishing memories that will foster our relationship into the future) for my Joy-Wealth lifestyle. Here's the thing: you need to know what you want out of your life to reach a level of Joy-Wealth. Moreover, you need to pursue this with a single-minded vision. All of this is true, but at the end of the day, you need human relationships to achieve Joy-Wealth. In the real world, material things may bring temporary pleasure, but the people in our lives are the true assets that we all need to acquire and cultivate. You can master the Material-Wealth process as I did, but there's no real success, no satisfaction to be gained when you lose everyone and everything you care about in the bargain, including yourself.

No matter how much your bank account may contain or how many things you collect, personal isolation and estrangements are crippling forms of poverty that can't be overcome by more accumulation or consumption. You can't buy a meaningful life because you can't attract positive, nurturing people into your life with nothing more than the newest thing or shiny object. For that, you need to build up your capital of personal character. You have to be a good person to attract good people.

Too often, people think that they have to wait until they've accumulated a certain amount of money and resources before they can live these principles. "If I'm going to take my kids on a trip, it has to be to the most expensive theme park" or "If I'm going to spend time with my family, we have to fly here or there and have the most amazing accommodations." Thus, they wait while they work and save, but they miss out on the opportunities that are right before them (current wealth). I'm not suggesting that there's no place for an amazing vacation or special occasion, but the amenities don't determine the degree of joy generated in those moments. Don't wait, and don't deny yourself. If you want, you can have a picnic at the park or a staycation at home with the family right now. The important part isn't where you go but how you spend the time together. The quality of these interactions will generate good times (current wealth) and enrich your relationships to generate happy memories for years to come (forecasted wealth).

These human connections offer an endless reservoir of joy and opportunities to exponentially increase joy not only in our own lives but also in the lives of those with whom we're connected. The more joy we bring to others, the more joy we have within ourselves. If you foster this symbiotic reaction both in managing your current wealth and investing in your forecasted wealth, then the inevitable result is an inexhaustible abundance of joy and satisfaction. That's true wealth. Joy-Wealth.

# CHAPTER NINETEEN

## The Most Important Wedge in the Wealth Pie

When assembling their Wealth Pie, most people are inclined to turn to what they consider to be the most important components of their lives—usually, their families. I understand that sentiment, but it's ultimately a misguided one.

Of course, family, friends, and business are all important. As I've made clear, my family is the primary source of joy in my own life. Nevertheless, I gave a lot of thought to the order in which each wedge of the Wealth Pie should appear in this book. For example, considering my personal Wealth Pie, I could argue that the family wedge is the most treasured or that the business wedge represents a fundamental component.

I considered a number of other options and then settled on the obvious choice for what would appear as the first wedge in our discussion.

Your Wealth Pie won't look like anyone else's. You'll have a completely different take on what's important to maximize joy in your life, what resources you have to invest in each sector, and what your expectations are for your returns.

No matter how different your Wealth Pie might be from mine or how either might evolve over the years, there's one category that everyone will share and which should always be a part of everyone's Wealth Pie.

For me, this isn't necessarily the most important wedge in my Wealth Pie or the one that brings me the most joy. Still, I acknowledge it as a fundamental piece for success in all other areas of my personal investments.

It's the wedge that represents me. I call it my "I" wedge: the "I" in Wealth Pie.

I've already described how I was once overwhelmed by guilt every time I took time away from my businesses to attend to another element of my life. I often made taking time for my wife, children, and family unnecessarily difficult as a way to justify taking any time at all. Likewise, I was grateful for the opportunities to serve my community but worried that these worthwhile endeavors were taking away from my business. Although I love my friends, I felt particularly guilty when I took time out of my day to enjoy their company—no matter how badly I needed to have a little bit of fun.

All of these troubled feelings combined were absolutely nothing compared to what I felt in those moments when I actually did something just for myself. In fact, the prospect of taking some time for myself was so difficult that I eventually stopped doing anything that I wanted to do for myself. I had no time for the gym because I had to be in the office extra early. I had no time to watch a movie that only I wanted to see because spending time with my family was more important. There was no time to travel, read, or think. In short, there was no time for me to be me.

While there were consequences from all of the faulty investments I made with my time and energy, such as distance from my family and isolation from my friends, I don't think anything was as damaging to me during this period as the time and energy I diverted from myself.

Without exercise, I felt increasingly worse physically until eventually, I was feeling slow and sluggish all of the time. Deprived of the opportunity to pursue my other interests, the monotony of business began to grind on me, and ironically, this began to erode the joy I'd always found in my work. All of this had a cumulative effect that continued to worsen exponentially until I finally felt that I was losing my sense of self.

I was troubled by my family and friends looking at me like a stranger, but I think the most disturbing realization for me at that time was that I was losing the ability to recognize myself.

That's when I absolutely knew that I had to change … or lose myself for good.

## The Selflessness of Selfishness and the Selfishness of Selflessness

Life is filled with little ironies. Looking back at myself during those dark days when I was slipping away from everyone, I believed that I wasn't choosing myself over others. On the contrary, I thought that I was being selfless in my approach to life. I didn't see myself as solely pursuing my own goals. Instead, I was making the necessary sacrifices to be a better husband, father, son, friend, and—just as importantly—employer for all of those who I knew relied on me and the businesses that I was growing.

I wasn't indulging myself; I was making sacrifices. Or so I thought.

Looking back on those days, I know it's an easy trap to fall into. We all know people who make sacrifices and then regard that gesture as a noble act. However, what they're really doing is promoting themselves. I think there's a strong connection to the victim complex there: "Look how much I'm doing for others. That's why I can't do anything for myself."

This is nonsense and perhaps the most selfish thing you can do.

Consider my situation. By depriving myself of what I needed to be happy, healthy, and whole, I wasn't a better CEO or family man. If I hadn't stopped myself from falling into that pit of despair, what would have become of all of those who depended on me?

There's a reason for the instructions announced aboard a jetliner before takeoff: "In case of an event in which the cabin loses air pressure, oxygen masks will be deployed. Be sure to secure your own mask before assisting others." That's not a provision for self-preservation but the smartest way to handle that sort of crisis—and your life.

The reasoning behind those instructions is that if you pass out while you're trying to help someone else, you can't help anyone, and two people need saving now. On the other hand, with your own oxygen supply securely in place, you can assist anyone else in need.

The same principle applies in life. Still, I frequently see people working to accomplish their goals while stubbornly trying to drag others along with them. I understand the sentiment, but I have to criticize the execution or lack thereof. If you can't take care of yourself, you can't take care of anyone else. Once you've established and positioned yourself to reach your goals, then you can reach out to take care of others.

Sometimes, the most selfless thing you can do is be selfish. Conversely, often, the most selfish thing you can do is be selfless.

If you want to maximize your life experiences, you must realize that it begins by strengthening and improving yourself.

## Spirituality

As I've said, I'm a businessman, and my feet are firmly planted in this world. My heart and soul are a different matter.

Islam frees my mind from the stress and anxiety of this world. It fills my heart with the courage to face any challenge and offers me Allah's grace in this world and the next. My faith forms the pillars of my life. It's the framework upon which my every day is built, and therefore, it's a key element in maximizing my life experiences. It's my belief in Islam that inspires me to be a better man. In fact, my faith forms the basis for everything that I've written here.

I can't imagine facing my day without the many benefits that I derive from my faith, and I certainly wouldn't have been able to achieve the level of self-improvement that I've realized over the years by following the Joy-Wealth Mindset.

My faith is firmly grounded in Islam, but I recognize that others may have their own. I respect that, of course. However, I strongly recommend that you explore your spirituality as a part of this program. While everyone should do so in their own private and personal way, I believe that you can't fully embrace your humanity without incorporating some aspect of spirituality.

## Your Mental State Is Physical

As we've discussed so far and will continue to do so, your mental state is at the heart of all of this, from recommitting your life to maximizing the joy that you experience in your life. Everything that we've discussed requires you to act with intention, and that's formed with the proper mindset.

As we discuss how to get into this frame of mind, you should understand that your every thought is a physical phenomenon at its core. Because of this, being in the right state of mind requires you to be in the right physical state.

Your mindset *is* your physical state.

## PHYSICAL FUNDAMENTALS

**Physical exam:** With any attempt to address your physical condition, such as a diet, exercise program, or anything of that nature, I suggest you begin your efforts by undergoing a physical exam by a licensed physician to assess your physical condition and needs, establish a baseline for measuring progress, and identify specific conditions that might need to be directly addressed to restore you to a fundamental level of health.

**Diet:** I'm not talking about losing weight simply for cosmetic purposes, although that may be something that you might want to undertake to reach your maximum result. What I'm talking about here is feeding your body with healthy and nutrient-rich foods while avoiding foods that contain toxic components. Your body needs a naturally sourced diet to function properly. Heavily processed foods have been proven to contribute not only to physical diseases but also to mental health issues. At the same time, you should maintain a positive mental state.

There are a thousand different diet plans and just as many considerations that you may want to factor into your plan. If they're available to you, I strongly recommend that you contact a health professional specializing in nutrition to design a diet that will allow you to optimize your physical health. If such resources aren't available to you, then by all means, you should take full advantage of the wealth of information available on the subject, create a healthy eating plan, and then stick to it.

**Hydration:** I'm not joining the crusade that's made the designer water bottle the must-have accessory. I'm merely pointing out that science has proven that not being properly hydrated can cause physical complications, such as sluggishness and circulation issues, and significantly reduce mental acuity.[19]

The proper level of hydration will vary from individual to individual and depend on a variety of conditions, but a rule of thumb is to shoot for drinking about two liters of clean water every day to ensure that you stay hydrated. And yes, this means that those who try to get it out of the way by drinking their daily quotient within a short period aren't getting the optimal benefit of this practice.

**Sleep:** For much of my life, going without sleep was a badge of honor and a declaration of my dedication to my business and the greater goal. Back in those days, we all bragged about how long it had been since we'd last been to bed. We blithely said, "I'll sleep when I'm dead."

Since those days, science has made it abundantly clear that missing even a single night of sleep can have a devastating impact on your physical and mental health and that prolonged sleep deprivation will kill you.[20] That's an extreme scenario, but what's very real is that most adults require a minimum of seven hours of sleep per day. Any deficit can have significant physical and mental con-

---

19 Pruthvi Shalum, "Effects of Dehydration on Cognitive Performance," iCliniq, September 26, 2023, https://www.icliniq.com/articles/emotional-and-mental-health/effects-of-dehydration-on-cognitive-performance.

20 Crystal Raypole, "Not Sleeping Probably Won't Kill You, but Things Will Get Ugly," Healthline, April 28, 2020, https://www.healthline.com/health/can-you-die-from-lack-of-sleep.

sequences, including reduced capacity to deal with stress, compromised memory, and foggy thinking—all of which are detrimental to successful performance during the day, not to mention maximizing your life experiences.[21]

We once thought that we were demonstrating our dedication, toughness, and willingness to make sacrifices by going without sleep, but what we were actually doing was compromising our performance in every aspect. Don't do that.

Maximizing your life starts with maximizing yourself, and getting enough sleep is fundamental to achieving that result.

**Exercise:** A trip to the gym was once thought of as part of looking a certain way. However, science has proven that exercise, including stretching, is essential to a healthy body. More than that, physical exercise is necessary for a healthy mind.

A regular exercise program is so important to your mental and emotional well-being that there's significant scientific research to support the assertion that regular exercise is more effective in treating depression than any of the drugs that are prescribed to treat the condition.[22] Regular exercise releases endorphins and other biochemicals that not only increase your level of pleasure afterward but also reward you with a feeling of well-being throughout the day and a sound sleep at night.

Again, countless exercise programs are available, but I strongly recommend that you contact a trainer or other professional to design a training program specifically for you and your individual fitness goals. Short of that, there are plenty of reputable resources on the internet that

21 Cleveland Clinic, "Here's What Happens When You Don't Get Enough Sleep," May 29, 2024, https://health.clevelandclinic.org/happens-body-dont-get-enough-sleep.

22 Robby Berman, "Is Exercise More Effective Than Medication for Depression and Anxiety?," MedicalNewsToday, March 3, 2023, https://www.medicalnewstoday.com/articles/is-exercise-more-effective-than-medication-for-depression-and-anxiety.

can provide you with all of the information that you need. Find a fitness routine that's so rewarding that it becomes a natural part of each day. Of course, you should always have a medical checkup for a physician's evaluation and clearance before you begin any exercise program.

## Tying It All Together

Those are the bare minimum fundamentals that you need to have in place to maximize your physical health and mental state.

One final thought: taking care of yourself physically is the ultimate statement of self-respect. A sound physical state and healthy body can't be bought; it's earned only through commitment and discipline. Your results are a direct reflection of your level of commitment and therefore one of the most authentic representations of what you bring to the table in all aspects of your life.

For all of these reasons, you must take care of yourself.

Maintaining proper healthcare, eating a healthy diet, hydrating adequately, getting sufficient sleep, and exercising regularly are the non-negotiable fundamentals of the lifestyle that you need to maintain to maximize your life experience investments. Meeting every one of these basic needs must become a regular part of your day if you're going to prepare yourself for a life of true wealth.

This means balancing the discipline of turning good habits into healthy routines and moderation in all things to enjoy yourself once in a while.

There will be occasions when you should go ahead and indulge in a decadent dining experience or put off a trip to the gym to spend some extra time at home with your family. This sort of flexibility is a necessity for living your best life and maximizing your life experience investment.

At the same time, you need to remind yourself that when it comes to habits, it's easier to break them than to make them. Before you know it, a night of overindulging can become a regular occurrence and a day away from the gym can quickly turn into a month. Be flexible, but be vigilant.

Be aware from the start that taking care of yourself isn't as hard as you think. Don't overcomplicate things. You have to get to a place where a physical fitness protocol that works for you feels effortless and joyful. Safeguarding your health, eating cleanly, hydrating, sleeping, and exercising are all fundamental practices that need to be incorporated into your daily routine so that you can fulfill these obligations whether you feel like it or not.

## A Little Bit More

While those are the personal investment fundamentals, a few additional practices can also be extremely beneficial.

### MINDFULNESS

Some people might call this section "meditation," but I think that term is limiting in the way it conjures up preconceived notions of a practice that's often misunderstood. While many people benefit from a structured form of meditation, science has made clear that a formal practice isn't necessary to gain the many benefits of mindfulness.

Any activity that allows you to focus on the present moment and temporarily withdraw from the chatter of your "monkey brain" and your day-to-day stressors will deliver significant benefits. These mindfulness activities can include a period of prayer, a quiet walk in nature, a moment of focused breathing, or a mantra of affirmation. When practiced regularly, any of these activities can deliver significant benefits to your physical and mental well-being. A regular mindfulness practice has been shown to boost cognition, improve emotional regulation—including regulating depression and anxiety—and lower blood pressure.[23]

However you choose to incorporate a mindfulness practice into your life, daily practice is an important addition to your overall fitness regimen.

## JOURNALING

Likewise, science has established that developing a practice of regularly recording your thoughts and feelings can have enormous physical and mental benefits, including stress reduction, moderation of negative thinking, and an overall improved feeling of well-being.[24]

Like meditation, one of the best things about journaling is that one form isn't necessarily better than another. The majority of studies on the subject have concluded that it doesn't matter whether you write, record, or sketch your thoughts and feelings. Whichever method you choose, the essential factor is the act of transferring your inner thoughts to a third-party medium.[25]

Again, the habituality over an extended period is responsible for the benefits derived from journaling, and the most important aspect of generating these beneficial effects is incorporating them into a regular part of your daily routine.

---

23 Nancy Lovering, "What Is Mindfulness?," PsychCentral, September 8, 2023, https://psychcentral.com/health/what-is-mindfulness#benefits.

24 Margarita Tartakovsky, "6 Journaling Benefits and How to Start Right Now," Healthline, February 22, 2022, https://www.healthline.com/health/benefits-of-journaling.

25 Margarita Tartakovsky, "6 Journaling Benefits and How to Start Right Now."

## BREATHING

Have you ever experienced a particularly disturbing crisis that sent you into a panic, only for someone to tell you to simply breathe?

I admit that for the longest time, I regarded this as one of the least helpful things a person could say to someone amid a personal crisis. Frankly, I've always found that particular instruction to be more than a little patronizing, as if it were minimizing the seriousness of my situation.

However, there may be a good deal of science behind that instruction.

There's a far more complicated explanation behind this that you can explore if you wish, but for our purposes, it's sufficient to know that when your body undergoes a sudden shock or stress, your breathing becomes quicker but shallower. This is a product of the fight-or-flight response, which speeds up your breathing rate to get more oxygen into your system.[26]

This is one of our most effective evolutionary adaptations, but it doesn't always serve us well in modern times.

With the sort of pressure that we all encounter today, the stresses we face often last longer than a predator's sudden charge that triggered our prehistoric ancestors. As a result, we experience extended bouts of shallow breathing, which deny our bodies a steady supply of oxygen over time. Our bodies interpret this as asphyxiation and go into a panic mode of their own, thus heightening the anxiety we're already experiencing. Increasing anxiety continues to interfere with our breathing, which worsens the anxiety—a perpetual cycle.

As a tip, if you're experiencing a bout of anxiety, try box breathing, a technique utilized by many, including some military operators.

---

26 Rajvi Desai, "Stress Has Made Us Shallow Breathers. Here's What It Does to Our Bodies," The Swaddle, August 28, 2020, https://www.theswaddle.com/stress-has-made-us-shallow-breathers-heres-what-it-does-to-our-bodies.

Breathe in deeply for a count of four, hold for a count of four, exhale for a count of four, hold for a count of four, and repeat the pattern. After a few cycles, your body will completely readjust itself to your situation, the cycle of anxiety will be interrupted, and you'll be on better footing for moving ahead.

More than just controlling your breath in stressful moments, there are benefits to be gained from regular breathing exercises. In addition to the anxiety and stress reduction benefits described above, regular breathing practice can provide a variety of benefits, including improving your overall respiratory system, regulating your nervous system, and improving attention and cognition.[27]

## And Beyond: Additional Practices

In addition to these practices, there are other protocols that you can incorporate into your daily routine. Cold exposure, such as cold plunges and cold showers, has been proven to have significant physical and mental benefits in terms of reducing inflammation, increasing fat loss, improving the metabolic system, improving cognition, and strengthening stress resistance.[28]

On the other end of the spectrum, saunas and other heat-related therapies have been shown to significantly improve overall health in numerous ways,[29] including inhibiting the development of

27 Daniela Ramirez-Duran, "The Power of Deep Breathing: 7 Techniques and Exercises," PositivePsychology, July 28, 2020, https://positivepsychology.com/deep-breathing-techniques-exercises/.

28 Tim Skwiat, "9 Health Benefits of Cold Exposure" BioTRUST, accessed July 2024, https://blog.biotrust.com/9-health-benefits-cold-exposure/.

29 Harvard Health Publishing, "Sauna Health Benefits: Are Saunas Healthy or Harmful?" May 14, 2020, https://www.health.harvard.edu/staying-healthy/saunas-and-your-health.

some cancers,[30] impeding the development and onset of age-related dementia and Alzheimer's disease, and treating depression.[31]

Science and holistic studies are regularly producing new methodologies for self-improvement, with new practices and modalities as close as your curiosity. I encourage you to use this as a starting point in your search for specific practices that provide optimal benefits for you and maximize your life experience.

This brings me to the final piece of the "I" wedge.

## Purpose and Passion

I no longer regret my difficult experiences back in those dark days when I sat alone in my well-appointed office, exhausted from overwork and sinking ever further into a seemingly bottomless pit of despair. Instead, I view them as the beginning of my rebirth.

I resolved then to change the course I'd plotted for myself, redeem myself, and make the best version of myself that I could be. This promise has turned into more than just a quest; it's my passion and drive in everything I do.

I threw myself into self-improvement with absolute commitment and the same sort of passion that I'd previously thought was only possible in pursuit of my business goals. I read books that I never would have encountered, which opened my eyes to a world beyond my own. I traveled the world and met amazing people and experts on a thousand different subjects. This process transformed me and made me a better man—the best man that I could be.

30 Susan Silberstein, "6 Ways Saunas Help Fight Cancer," BeatCancer.org, October 31, 2014, https://beatcancer.org/blog/6-ways-saunas-help-fight-cancer/.

31 Leigh Ann Tahami, "6 Ways Saunas Can Reduce Symptoms Of Depression," The Accrescent, accessed July 2024, https://www.theaccrescent.com/saunas-depression/.

Most importantly, my journey gave me something that everyone needs in their life: a reason not just to get out of bed but to *spring* out of bed. People need more than just a job or a career objective. They have to have something that fulfills a sense of purpose within them, something they're passionate about—because passion is life.

Don't get me wrong, my wife and children are my reason to spring out of bed—my businesses and friends too. But everyone needs their own source of passion.

You can't live your life for anyone other than yourself. This means you need to have something for yourself. This is the opposite of being selfish; it's being selfless. The object of your passion doesn't matter. The important element is having a purpose that fills you with satisfaction at the end of the day and inspires you for the next day.

## And Maybe One More Thing

You should also have some form of relaxation that's just for you. As I mentioned earlier, for me, it's watching movies, particularly documentaries. This doesn't mean that my wife's selections don't dominate our date nights or that I'm not there for whatever animated treasure the kids want to watch. However, I regularly take the opportunity to have some time alone when I can relax by myself and watch *The Last Dance* for the forty-seventh time or some other film just for me.

You have to leave some time for yourself to travel and explore the world, even if it's just going for a walk sometimes. It's also essential to allow yourself the chance to clear your mind and strategize without any interference from the outside world. More than anything, you must give yourself the space to be free and at ease with the world.

You have to take care of and be kind to yourself, and this includes how you talk to yourself. If you're fighting yourself, how can you ever expect to win?

Think of it this way: if you don't take care of yourself, then no one else will. Furthermore, if you're taking from yourself constantly without replacing your supply or repairing yourself, then sooner or later, you're going to bottom out. You won't be of use to anyone then.

You have to love yourself.

And sometimes, in order to be selfless, you have to be selfish.

# CHAPTER TWENTY

## The Family Wedge

For me—and likely for many others—the family wedge is the core wedge in the Wealth Pie. Even when I was caught up in my race for riches and wasn't as present as I probably should have been for my family, my love for them has always been and continues to be the driving force in my life. There's no doubt that I wanted to achieve certain goals in my businesses, and I don't deny that there was an assortment of things that I was happy to add to my collections, but my efforts in those days were never about me—not really.

I wanted to provide for my wife and guarantee that my children would never lack anything and be able to fully enjoy the future that they deserve. I wanted to make my parents and all of my family proud of the man I'd grown up to be. I wanted to live up to the legacy of excellence that comes with the Batterjee name and honor all of those who'd borne it before me through the generations.

All of these considerations continue to be of the utmost importance to me. I'm not talking about altering these sources of motivation but rather changing how I go about incorporating them into my life in the most productive way possible.

Family is a sweeping term that needs to be broken down into three sections: spouses/significant others, parents/children, and extended family.

## Marriage

To the northwest of Riyadh, the stark beauty of endless slopes of sand gives way to a geological miracle: a sheer wall of sandstone. Known as *Jebel Fihraynd* or "Edge of the World," the rock face rises three hundred meters (about a thousand feet) above the desert landscape and provides an unrestricted view of the curvature of the Earth into the horizon.

While the site has been a source of inspiration for individuals in the region for thousands of years, it's only recently gained the attention of a growing number of rock climbers from within Saudi Arabia and around the world.

I hope that you don't have a fear of heights because I want you to imagine yourself as one of those rock climbers making their ascent up the face of the Edge of the World. Picture yourself halfway up the rock face with a long climb ahead of you and nothing but five hundred meters of air and the desert floor beneath you. One wrong move, one lost footing, and … well, you know.

I don't want you to think that I'd leave you there all alone. No, I want you to add another climber to this scenario: someone tethered to you so that their actions can help or hinder your progress up the rock face, and any issues with them could spell disaster for you both.

I want you to picture a climbing partner to whom your future and fate are literally tied.

If you had the opportunity to choose this partner, how would you go about it? Would you choose your fellow climber based on whether they were wearing designer climbing gear, or would you opt for someone who knew how to climb? Would you rather have the partner that all of the other climbers want to join their expeditions, or would you pick the climber who knew the ascent route and was dedicated to seeing you make your way to the top?

Once you've made your selection, consider for a moment how you'd treat that person on your ascent. Would you ignore your partner on your tethered ascent and continue to climb as if you were solo and untethered? Would you undermine their efforts, not caring whether their fall meant your untimely descent to the ground below?

I think it's safe to say that if you were tasked with climbing the treacherous rock face of the Edge of the World, you'd choose a partner based on their climbing ability and their likeliness to assist you on your climb to the top. Once you begin your ascent up that sheer sheet of sandstone, I'm sure you'll recognize the importance of taking care of and cooperating with your climbing partner.

Marriage is a tandem ascent up a rock face.

Everything that I've included on these pages is about creating a life that's fulfilling to you as an individual. I've written about the need to acknowledge and accommodate your authentic self, as well as the selflessness of selfishness. I continue to stand behind all of that.

At the same time, living a life that maximizes your sense of joy and fulfillment is based on incorporating and developing your relationships with others. While maintaining your individuality is important, a satisfying life is dependent on developing healthy relationships with others. Nowhere is that truer than creating a marriage or primary personal relationship.

While your individual performance is the crucial determinant in your overall life satisfaction, I don't think it's possible to overstate the proposition that your marriage or primary relationship is the foundational relationship of your life.

A good marriage that operates as a true partnership and in which both parties are working synergistically to accomplish shared goals will offer you much-needed support in all of your endeavors. By contrast, an ill-suited marriage can be devastating and drain energy and resources from all of your other endeavors, which can prove nearly impossible to overcome over time.

## IF YOU'RE STILL SINGLE

Because of the importance of finding a suitable and supportive partner, choosing a spouse should be considered one of the most important undertakings of your life. That's not to say that there's not a time for enjoying yourself during a stage of your life, but the serious business of choosing a life partner should be approached the same way as you would a significant investment.

### *Don't Fall for the Surface*

I acknowledge that we're talking about human and not financial relationships here, but the premise is the same. You wouldn't buy a house based solely on curb appeal or purchase a car solely from catalog pictures. That seems almost too elementary to write down for an adult readership, but I'm always surprised by the number of young couples that I meet who seem to have nothing in common except an attraction to superficial considerations.

The fact of the matter is that choosing a life partner is far too crucial a decision to be relegated to such a shallow criterion. Understand, too, that these types of factors—although understandably attractive—are temporary and will change over time. There's no sense in entering into a lifelong contract based on temporary considerations.

*Do Your Due Diligence*

Just as with any substantial investment, a potential life partnership deserves deep scrutiny, including learning about the other person, understanding expectations, and examining track records. There's no reason for a couple to go through all the steps of getting married and then realize afterward that they aren't on the same page about raising their children, can't agree on financial planning, or don't share the same life ambitions as a couple.

While the courtship period is undoubtedly a thrill all its own, it's important to take the process seriously. A deep conversation or two to determine long-term compatibility can save years of unnecessary acrimony.

## IF YOU'RE MARRIED

My relationship with my wife is one of the most important elements in my life. She's a source of joy for me. Rather than take this for granted, I intentionally take steps to put these feelings into action as a way to maximize the joy that I experience with her in every precious moment.

Telling you that I'm committed to this as a daily practice shouldn't be written off as mere romanticism. As with everything else that I've shared with you, there's a practical purpose here. Fostering and strengthening my marital relationship has the effect of empowering me in every aspect of my life.

Because your primary personal partnership is as important—if not more so—than your business relationships, you should maintain and protect it with greater vigilance. In short, if you're married, then the smartest thing you can do is treat this union as the most important partnership in your life and take the necessary steps to make it as productive as possible.

This means looking at your behavior and contributions to the union.

When I was deep in my race for riches, I would have told you that my wife was one of my primary motivators. I was working all of the time, but in my heart and head, I was working for her. Furthermore, I'd convinced myself that she was aware of these motivations. We didn't discuss the situation; I assumed that we shared this understanding. It never dawned on me that she might see my driving ambition as anything else.

The fact remained that I wasn't as present as I needed to be.

One of the most important things about maximizing joy is being present. I don't mean that in the physical sense, although that's important too. What I'm talking about is being present in the relationship. There's a natural tendency to take things for granted, including the people who matter to us most.

The first step is to initiate and maintain an open line of communication. I assumed that my wife understood that she was my prime motivation without making that clear to her. However, I failed to communicate how difficult those times were, and I don't believe she fully understood the tremendous stressors that were dragging me down.

If most people tried to conduct their businesses with the level of communication that they put into their marriages, they'd soon understand the need for more open channels at home. This includes respectfully communicating which of your needs aren't being met in the relationship and how that deficit might be addressed.

Next, I invite you to take an inventory of all of the things that you can do to improve your relationship. That's not an easy thing to do, but it's necessary. It's funny that people are constantly reviewing their business performance and looking for input to make themselves better executives, but they never apply the same protocols to their personal relationships.

Taking practical steps to improve your primary relationship maximizes your joy and strengthens all aspects of life. The more synchronized you are, the easier your climb and the more satisfying the view from the top.

## Children

Throughout this book, we've talked about the need for balance in your life, but if there's one area of life where I think any of us are tempted to go to the extreme, it's our relationships with our children. I think this is true because the love we feel for our children is often not only the strongest force that we'll ever feel but the most complicated. We're usually ready to accept irregularities in our other relationships; however, it's natural for us as parents to want to make our children's lives perfect—and that's where everything can go wrong.

Let me share a short story with you. Picture yourself walking in the woods on a spring day. Imagine finding a butterfly that has just emerged from its chrysalis stage and is struggling to free itself from the confines of its cocoon.

Because your heart is filled with empathy, you take out a pocketknife and carefully set about cutting the butterfly free from its silk prison. You want to make everything perfect for the little butterfly, right?

While you mean the best for the butterfly, what you fail to take into consideration is that it's the process of escaping the cocoon that allows it to strengthen its wings in preparation for taking flight. Without the benefit of that struggle, the butterfly is unable to fly on its own and can never live an independent life.

That's how simple your relationship with your children can be. Give them the love and support that they need as they go through the difficult process of learning how to fly on their own.

When I was racing after riches, I thought that I was doing everything I could to provide the best possible life for my children. I told myself that the positions I obtained and the things that I achieved would set them up for lives in which they had everything and wouldn't have to know any struggles. Everything that I did was meant to improve their lives.

What I didn't understand was that I was depriving them of what they needed the most: a father who was present for them. I was trying to help them but unknowingly depriving them of what they needed most to learn how to fly.

When I began to consider my role as a parent with true intention, I recognized that what mattered most to them wasn't the things that I could give them or the benefits I could provide. It was the time that I spent with them.

In turn, spending time with them was what heightened my joy as well.

Since I've redefined wealth and created a special piece of my Wealth Pie to represent my children, I make a point of servicing that obligation every day. My daily schedule doesn't just include business meetings and site visits. There's also an allotment for time in the pool with the kids. If I have to take a call on a weekend, it's likely to be pushed back. Or, I wait until after my children are put to bed for the night, and I'm free to redirect my attention from them.

I do this because what our children need most—the only thing they need, really—is to know that they have their parents' love, attention, and support. While the process of growing up is never easy, with the knowledge that they matter in this world—especially to their parents—every child will find a way to spread their wings and fly.

Watching your children learn to fly on their own may be the ultimate way to increase your joy.

## Parents

In Islam, the term for taking care of one's parents is *birr al-walidayn*, which means "being dutiful to parents." While this sacred duty is a part of my religion, I believe it's an essential exercise for anyone who wishes to live the Joy-Wealth lifestyle.

As I write this, I'm in the middle of designing and creating a new project in the emerging well-being sphere. As part of the planning stage, I had the privilege of meeting a well-known and highly regarded architect. We arranged to get together for coffee one Friday morning. When we met, I noticed that the man seemed to be glowing with a radiant sense of peace.

"I feel so humble and blessed," he told me.

Because our meeting was about developing a project focused on well-being—a subject that fascinates me—I assumed that his elevated state must have been the result of a new cutting-edge technique. But when I asked him to explain, he told me, "My work puts so much pressure on me that I was feeling completely exhausted and overwhelmed. I called my mom, who lives in a quieter area of Saudi, known for palm trees and dates. I went and stayed with her for a week; no calls or meetings, just me being fully present with my mother. I could have gone to any spa or resort, but just a week with my mother in this rural location did far more for my body, mind, and soul. Just being able to talk to my mother one on one, the simplicity and ease of that life, relieved my stress and renewed my vitality completely."

I understood what he'd undergone because I've also made a point of spending time with my parents to access that special sense of security and peace. I regularly spend time with my mother, not only to show my respect to her for everything that she's done for me but also to benefit from her wisdom and calming presence. We travel together—just the two of us—and it's always a wonderful experience to be able to spoil someone who did so much for me and made me the man that I am.

My father is a great man who's still very much involved in the business world. We connect on that level, and I can't overstate the importance of not only picking the brain of such an accomplished businessman but also having an interchange with my dad.

Your relationship with your parents reflects on your wife, your children, and everyone around you because they realize that you have a soft, caring spot. It humbles you, and I believe this is an important component. The ego can be a dangerous thing if allowed to grow out of control. Family—particularly parents—has a way of reminding us of the children that we were. I'm a titan of business, but whenever I stand before my mother or father, I'm reminded that I'm always their son. This has had an extremely beneficial effect on me in terms of reminding me who I am. No matter what I achieve, I'll always be the son they named Sultan.

My relationship with my parents is part of acknowledging my origin, giving back what's been given to me, and demonstrating my loyalty.

A lot of people say, "I need to leave the house and pursue my dreams! No one knows more than I do, and I'm going to do my own thing!" While I understand the feeling, this sort of ambition needs to be balanced with these significant relationships and responsibilities. Part of being humble is being grateful, and part of being grateful is being able to relate to your roots. I'm reminded of the adage, "A tree never grows taller than its roots grow deep."

In terms of current wealth and forecasted wealth, your relationship with your parents forecasts your relationship with your children. You're teaching them how to treat their parents.

## Extended Family

I'm proud of the life I've built with my wife and our children, but our family is an extension of a larger family. We're building an addition to something bigger than us and creating something greater and more beautiful than the assembled individuals.

I love my family and my extended family, but when I was racing for riches, I saw and interacted with them less and less. I missed them all, but I was under the impression that by achieving personal success, I was adding to our legacy.

Later, when I took the time and made the intentional effort to redefine wealth and create my Wealth Pie, I set aside a significant wedge to represent the extended family that I hadn't been as involved in as I might have wanted. I concentrated on being a better son, brother, nephew, and uncle. I intentionally made a point of reconnecting with the people who meant so much to me.

Since I've focused with intention on the Joy-Wealth in my life, I've come to rethink my relationships with all of my family members—particularly my brothers and sisters. I think it's easy to take one's siblings for granted for no other reason than that they've always—or almost always—been a part of your life. And unlike your parents, they're not in a position of responsibility. They're sharing the same difficult journey to adulthood with you.

That's what's made me realize that my brothers and sisters and I have far more in common than our name and origin story. We share the same starting point and are forever cotravelers on this journey through life. Each of my brothers and sisters is a wonderful, flourishing adult in their own right, but what truly fills my heart with the most joy is to consider the amazing bond that ties us all. They're a constant source of love and support and a fundamental element of my most important family wedge.

In life, as reflected by the Wealth Pie, there's often a fine line between family and friends. I've already addressed the importance of friendship, but the trust and camaraderie we can develop with our siblings is like no other. I'm fortunate that my siblings and I not only share a familial bond, but we're also the best of friends. And in that way, the Joy-Wealth Mindset seeks to make the most of this fine line by creating the best of both worlds: making friends of our family and family of our friends.

When I was growing up, birthdays were observed but not necessarily celebrated. My birthday falls in August, and we were often traveling or on holiday when the occasion came around. Recently, I marked a milestone birthday: my fortieth. I'd made a mental note but wasn't expecting any special attention. We were traveling as an extended family, and I didn't think there'd be an opportunity for anything more than a passing observation.

Imagine my surprise when every day of our vacation had a special birthday feature, such as an elaborate dinner party, an exquisite feast my wife had organized, and a birthday message created with flower petals on the path to the swimming pool.

I wasn't just overwhelmed by these gestures by all of those whom I love so much; I was struck by the realization of how much I'd missed—and would have continued to do without—during my race for riches.

My focus on honoring my family by achieving material success had failed to account for the contributions that I brought through my very human interactions not with my ancestors from the past but with my living family.

By prioritizing a piece of the family wedge in my Wealth Pie, I've managed to reconnect with my family and realized their importance in my life. They've not only brought true wealth to my life, but they've also given me a greater sense of my worth in a real way.

Later that year, my extended family went to Dubai for New Year's to celebrate the year that had passed and gather our energies for the future. During the festivities, one of my nephews turned to me and, out of the blue, said, "Congratulations."

I was taken aback. "For what?"

He seemed surprised, as if there was something I should have known. "You've been named one of the top CEOs in MENA. You're ranked number thirteen in Saudi Arabia." He took out his phone and showed me the article that had just been published in *Forbes*.

To say I was grateful would be a gross understatement—not only to *Forbes* for the recognition but also to my incredible teams whose collective contributions had helped me reach that position. It was undoubtedly an incredible honor and one that I'm enormously proud of, but I'll share with you a secret. When I was racing after riches, being included in such an illustrious list would have dominated my conversation for the remainder of the evening and probably the rest of the trip. However, I never mentioned the honor again that night—not because I didn't understand the far-reaching implications of such an honor but because what I felt most strongly at the time was gratitude for being able to share a greater moment with my family.

The joy I found in my love and appreciation for my family overcame any feelings of individual pride or triumph.

More than that, I was aware of a change in me and grateful for it too.

By incorporating the family wedge into my Wealth Pie, I was able to multiply the joy I experienced a thousandfold.

# CHAPTER TWENTY-ONE

## The Friend Wedge

Looking back at those dark days when I was lost in my obsession with being rich, through the corrective lenses of hindsight, I can see now that there were warning signs that I was getting close to crashing and burning. Still, I was mindful of the fact that with all that I'd sacrificed, abandoned, and given up on in my mad dash for riches, my tipping point was the phone that didn't ring.

I've come to think of that deafening silence as a wake-up call.

I'm fortunate to have an amazing circle of friends. Even during those days when all of my time was invested in growing my businesses and pursuing my ambitions, I never outgrew them or exchanged them for newer models. It wasn't that I didn't want to continue going out and having good times with them—just the opposite.

I felt guilty about spending time with my friends. In my mind, this was a selfish indulgence and an expenditure of time that might be better devoted to my businesses. I was already aware that I was shortchanging my family with my time and attention, and doing the same to my friends seemed like a misguided compensation for this. Sure, I was too busy for tuck-ins with my kids or family dinners, but I felt there was some kind of misdirected virtue in neglecting my friends as well. I came to think of any time that I spent with my friends as selfish and time away from them as a noble sacrifice I was making for the greater good.

Now, it strongly resonates with me that what was initially responsible for drawing my attention to my dire situation was the calls—or lack of calls—from my friends.

I'm fortunate to have a close circle of friends, most of whom go back to our earliest days. We've been through everything together. It might be accurate to say that they're more family than friends to me. As I write these words, it seems impossible that I could have considered time with them as anything other than very, very necessary to who I am and who I want to be.

There's a reason for this. Scientific research has proven that strong friendships are important to our survival and are responsible for producing all sorts of biochemicals that are essential to our well-being, including dopamine, serotonin, and oxytocin. Maintaining friendships is as important to our overall health as diet and exercise, and cultivating a friend group has been proven to extend life expectancy.[32]

Conversely, neglecting our human need for personal connections is actively detrimental to our well-being. The Harvard Study of Human Development, an ongoing study initiated in 1939, established that close human connections are the strongest links to happiness and more important to a sense of satisfaction in life than

32 Leah Mandel, "Why We Need Friends, According to a Scientist," Fader, March 8, 2017, https://www.thefader.com/2017/03/08/science-of-friendship.

social status, fame, and riches. Moreover, the study showed that loneliness and social isolation are as actively detrimental to one's physical health as smoking or alcoholism.[33] Additional studies have linked loneliness to increased risks of stroke, heart attack, obesity, and chronic or acute pain.[34]

As for the steep rise in anxiety and depression that we discussed at the beginning of the book, you guessed it: loneliness and the lack of a supportive friend network are the primary drivers of these mental health issues, along with other serious mental and emotional conditions.[35]

Going without friends is like going without food, water, exercise, or sleep.

I was fortunate to have learned this lesson. When we're focusing on generating Joy-Wealth in our lives, there are few sources greater than our friends.

Recently, all of my closest friends had plans to go out for a night on the town. However, phone calls regretfully passing on our plans started coming in that afternoon. Some had work commitments, while others had family obligations. Our big night out eventually came down to just me and another friend.

Our plans to go out seemed pointless for just us two, so we chose to spend the night talking by the pool in my backyard instead. We reminisced about things we hadn't thought about in many years—all of the wondrous adventures we'd undertaken as boys when life was so much simpler.

---

33 Vanessa Van Edwards, "7 Science-Backed Reasons Why Friends Are Important," accessed July 2024, https://www.scienceofpeople.com/friends-important/.

34 Sarah F. Allen et al., "The Associations between Loneliness, Social Exclusion and Pain in the General Population: A Cross-Sectional UK Biobank Study," *Journal of Psychiatric Research* 130 (2020): 68–74, https://doi.org/10.1016/j.jpsychires.2020.06.028.

35 World Economic Forum, "Harvard Researchers Discovered a Major Cause of Loneliness - and the Key to Fighting It," November 4, 2022, https://www.weforum.org/agenda/2022/11/loneliness-health-depression-mental-alone/.

We shared our thoughts on our adult lives too. Without the distractions of the nightlife, we got honest about all of the serious things that we have to deal with now that we've grown up.

By the end of the night, we reminded ourselves of the unbreakable bond that exists between us and those who were with us only in spirit. I couldn't help but look up at the stars overhead and feel a connection with all of those who'd also spent their evenings talking quietly beneath the evening sky and faced their lives together in the company of good friends. These sorts of connections with individuals and humanity are so important for cultivating Joy-Wealth in our lives.

A connection with someone else is very reassuring. Human relationships support all of us and give us meaning. When you can go back with someone to when you were a child and life was simple, it's a wonderful point of reference for what your life can be. It's easy to get caught up in the anxiety of it all when words get thrown around, but these people can ground you and keep you focused on what's important in a life based on Joy-Wealth.

This is true because joy begets joy, and the most effective way to bring joy into your life is to first bring joy to someone else.

I've told you already a bit about the friends' trip to Madrid that I organized to watch Real Madrid CF in the semifinals of the UEFA Champions League, but our adventure didn't start smoothly. When the prospect of the trip first hit me, I excitedly reached out to all of my closest friends, with details of a plan that was too good for them to pass on.

One by one, every one of them came back to me with "I'd really love to go, but ..."

Every one of their excuses was 100 percent legitimate, and I felt for them. However, I'm ferociously tenacious once I put my mind to an objective.

I did some quick math and got back to each of them. "Listen, the trip I'm planning will take four days. There are 365 days in the year. That's less than 1 percent of the year. Think about the return on time and investment here: 1 percent investment and the returns will be epic!"

One by one, the calls came in. "Count me in, I'm coming."

Once we made that collective decision, we had the best time planning our trip. The experience of boyhood friends banding together for another adventure was a source of joy for us all. The thrill of Madrid and the excitement of the crowd in the stadium—everything about the experience was joyful.

Here's the thing about joy: if my friends had listened to the negative voices in their heads telling them that they shouldn't go—something I understand from personal experience—then they would have spent the days of our trip brooding or maybe envying those who'd made the decision to go. That negativity would have spread through their lives and affected many with whom they came in contact.

When we returned from our wonderful holiday in Madrid, all of us were filled with gratitude for the friendship we shared and the joy of our adventure. Rather than being glum, my friends returned to their family and friends with joy, and they resumed their business with joy.

Joy has a unique capacity for building upon itself. It's like a rock thrown in a pool, making ripples. The more joy you put into the world (current wealth), the more joy you create for yourself and others (forecasted wealth).

Friendship is a wonderful and necessary wedge in anyone's Wealth Pie.

By investing in creating joy for others, you'll find there's a significant return on investment that comes back to you.

Around that same time, one of our friends had attained a major accomplishment. We organized a weekend adventure at Saudi Safari to celebrate. In Saudi Arabia, a safari more commonly features auto sports than the wild animals those outside the kingdom might commonly think of. Not to be outdone, my friends arranged to bring Bobcat skid-steer loaders, which are named after the big cat. My friends thought this was hilarious because I'm well known in the construction and real estate fields.

"Can you show us how to steer these?" They all laughed.

We had a wonderful time. We were a bunch of big kids playing in the world's greatest sandbox. Out in the wilderness, completely free from the day-to-day responsibilities that were very much a part of our high-achiever lifestyles, we bonded again in the joy of our friendship. No one enjoyed themselves more than I did.

Toward the end of our outing, as we were eating, my friends brought out a special cake to celebrate my being named by *Forbes* as a top-five CEO in the construction/real estate development industry in the kingdom. I was touched beyond words that my friend had chosen to include me in that way and made me feel that all of my efforts on behalf of our friendship had been appreciated and reciprocated.

Real friends celebrate and encourage one another's successes. I'm surrounded by real friends, and that fills my heart with joy.

By investing in my current wealth (i.e., regular activities with my friends), I'd also made an investment in my forecasted wealth (i.e., fostering friendships that paid dividends and would continue to do so).

However, as with everything else, this comes with some considerations.

I was out with my children when we bumped into an acquaintance whom I knew well enough and liked just fine. We chatted pleasantly for a minute or two and then went on our way. On the way home in the car, my daughter asked me, "Baba, was that man your friend?"

One of the many blessings of children is that they ask the simplest questions which hold within them the most complicated layers.

The man I'd spoken with was a great guy, and seeing him was a very welcome surprise, but I hesitated before I answered my daughter. Was he my friend?

"Yes," I replied. "And no."

I'll share with you the same explanation I gave my daughter.

There are friends, and then there are *friends*.

We all have people in our lives with whom we're friendly. Maybe we socialize and go out with them now and again. These are the people with whom we share some social connections. The British anthropologist Robin Dunbar published a paper suggesting that the maximum number of social contacts for most people is around 150: Dunbar's number. (Don't worry if you're particularly gregarious, as subsequent studies suggest that for some people, the number may be higher.[36])

But then, there are *friends*. A survey suggested that the number of people filling these roles in our lives is only three to five.[37] By *friends*, I mean people who are close to us and who we can rely on with some level of expected trust. To my mind, trust is the most important word here.

We all have people in our lives who are with us for parties and good times but forget us at the first sign of trouble. Worse, they may be keen to stir up trouble themselves. *Friends* are with you no matter

---

36 Stockholm University, "New Study Deconstructs Dunbar's Number - Yes, You Can Have More Than 150 Friends," May 4, 2021, https://www.su.se/english/news/new-study-deconstructs-dunbar-s-number-yes-you-can-have-more-than-150-friends-1.553823.

37 Sonya Matejko, "How Many Friends Do You Need?," PsychCentral, November 10, 2022, https://psychcentral.com/relationships/how-many-friends-do-you-need#how-many.

what. Ride or die. As I explained to my young daughter, both of these types of people are essential to living a full and satisfying life, but the distinction between the two is important.

The caveat here is that there's a big difference between a friend and a *friend*, and there are few emotional intelligence skills that are more important than being able to discern between the two.

A friend is someone with whom you can share a meal or a social event. They may be sources of good conversation or insight into a shared interest. However, they're not there for you, and they can't be trusted beyond those roles. That is, you can't trust them to have your back, and so you need to regard them with a degree of caution. They'll almost certainly leave you behind if you encounter any trouble.

Your *friends* are with you for life. You can confide in them and count on them to lend a hand or put their shoulder to your wheel when times get hard.

Confusing the two can be a disastrous mistake. I can't begin to count the number of times I've seen someone trust a person they thought was their *friend* but who turned out to be just a friend and burned them.

A *friend* is an extremely valuable asset, and you should do everything possible to keep them in your life and close to you. This includes returning the gift of friendship.

The key to having *friends* is to be a *friend* yourself, and this will require your time and energy. My *friends* were right to stop calling me when my obsessive race for riches reached a point at which I could no longer be a *friend* to them. Believe me, I recognize how fortunate I am that my time spent foolishly chasing riches didn't cost me the people I know are my *friends*.

Maintaining friendships is an essential part of life—physically and emotionally. As such, it deserves your time and energy.

As you're planning your investments and returns for your time, it's important to recognize the different levels of friendship. The more important a friendship is to you, the more it deserves your investment.

As I mentioned, a recent plan for a night out on the town fell apart until it was just me and one of my oldest friends. Although I always enjoy going out with these guys, it was wonderful to spend a quiet evening at home, talking to someone I've known for my entire life.

There's real value in these sorts of relationships, and they're well worth a wedge in your Wealth Pie.

# CHAPTER TWENTY-TWO

## Business and the Three Ps

I had the great fortune to grow up in a home that revolved around business. Some of my earliest memories are of being around my father and uncle as they discussed the deals that they were making or the projects they were developing. The whole process seemed magical and was fascinating to me even at an early age. Maybe most young boys dream of being superheroes or driving sports cars, but these men with their serious discussions about corporate maneuvers and building businesses were my role models for my future.

I don't think it's an exaggeration to say I was born into business. Running a corporation—or several of them, as I do—is all I've ever wanted to do with my life. Therefore, it should come as no surprise that the business wedge makes up a significant portion of my Wealth Pie.

## The Three Ps

Business is the area of my life in which it's easiest to introduce my pillars or the three Ps: purpose, passion, and persistence. I believe that all three are necessary elements of every aspect of one's life and that they should be incorporated into every wedge that makes up your individual Wealth Pie.

In terms of business, if you want to successfully embody a Joy-Wealth Mindset and achieve true wealth, then it's critical you apply the three Ps to your business.

**Purpose:** Everyone needs a reason not only to get up every morning but also to spring out of bed. Each of us must have something to drive us—a sense of purpose.

I've always found this sort of life-affirming purpose in my companies. Each of the businesses I run has a unique purpose, but above all of them is an overarching purpose to build valuable, quality projects that touch the lives of people and communities around the globe. Fulfilling that promise to ourselves, our clients, and our communities is the guiding force that regulates everything we do. For me, walking that well-defined path brings everything we do into alignment in terms of current wealth (i.e., our performance every day) and forecasted wealth (i.e., our strategic plan for development over time).

**Passion:** To fulfill this sense of purpose, it's not enough to go through the motions. I'm committed to each operation with everything that I've got. It's not merely a matter of profit and return. I've invested my heart and soul into every one of my companies, and I demand the same level of dedication from every single member of my teams. Nothing less will do. If you have true passion, you'll never work a day in your life.

This is reflected in my Wealth Pie in the time and energy I invest in each of my businesses. While my diagram accommodates the different wedges that make up my Joy-Wealth life, it also reflects my total commitment to my businesses.

**Persistence:** Any business is an inherently volatile and turbulent endeavor, given to seismic waves of highs and lows. If you're unprepared to weather the inevitable storms and continue on the course you've set, then your failure is assured. No matter how well defined your purpose is or how passionate you may be to reach its fulfillment, life will always offer you challenges and put stones in your path. If you don't have the power of persistence—the courage to continue no matter what obstacles you face—then you'll never be able to reach the goals you've set for yourself or realize the purpose you've adopted. Purpose and passion are essential, but they mean nothing if you're not prepared to persevere until you reach—or exceed—your objective.

All of this is true for business, but it applies to every other aspect of life as well. Each of the wedges in your Wealth Pie should have these elements incorporated into it. Whether we're talking about something as important as your relationship with your significant other or something secondary like your desire to achieve a level of accomplishment in one of your hobbies, you must possess and harness the full power of the three Ps.

If you've aligned your passion with your purpose and made a commitment to persevere, you can achieve anything that you want. This belief is foundational in my life.

Those who hold the Material-Wealth Mindset will inevitably wind up feeling hollow and empty despite their successes. They don't have a driving sense of purpose and deep passion to generate the steady source of joy that is at the center of true wealth.

I know this is true because my discovery of Joy-Wealth significantly changed my approach to doing business, how I look at my companies, and my long-term strategies for the future. I now view these corporations with absolute love, and this generates the joy and true wealth for which I'd always been searching. More than that, by creating my Wealth Pie and consistently working through the process, I've developed a way to stay grounded through gratitude, which empowers me to become a better businessman and more effective corporate leader.

Now when I'm reviewing my goals and meeting with the team leads of each of my corporations, I often incorporate the philosophy of *Be Your Own Sultan,* and our shared understanding of the need to find joy in the business touches everything that we do. We realize that by building healthcare and educational buildings, developing communities, and optimizing natural resources, we're impacting hundreds of thousands of lives directly and millions indirectly. This is the ultimate driver for us.

Each of us recognizes how lucky we are to be in a field where we design and build structures that will create a chain of impacts with diverse groups of people, encompassing suppliers, employees, end users, and their families. We're grateful for these opportunities, from the current wealth perspective (i.e., the immediate effect we have on people) to the forecasted wealth outlook (i.e., the value we're creating for generations to come). This philosophy has helped me greatly in managing my teams and aligning them with the three Ps of business.

I'm working smarter than ever before, and my teams are right with me in terms of maximized productivity. We aren't just mentally present in our work; we're emotionally engaged, which has transformed how we do business across the board. Each of my companies has taken on my personal energy and become appreciatively more dynamic. By any metric, the benefits of our collective efforts to adopt the Joy-Wealth Mindset and apply the principles of *Be Your Own Sultan* (BYOS) are undeniable throughout my organizations. Simply put, Joy-Wealth has made us all better businesspeople.

This doesn't mean that we don't continue to work long hours. But because we're guided by the process of managing our individual Wealth Pies rather than blindly putting in the time, we're far more productive and better positioned to achieve more favorable results. Because we're aware of our position in terms of current wealth and know where we want to be with our forecasted wealth, we approach our businesses more strategically in this rapidly changing marketplace. This allows me to redefine our goals as needed from a human capital point of view. It also affords me the opportunity to decide who I want to do business with, the business issues I need to focus on, and how to plan my course from there.

Adopting the BYOS philosophy has allowed me to play the game a step ahead of others. I'm able to play where the ball is going, not where it is today. This has allowed me to effortlessly be in the right place at the right time to foster the growth and development of all of my businesses in ways that I never could have previously imagined.

Adopting the Joy-Wealth Mindset and integrating the three Ps into your Wealth Pie take time, but it can quickly shift your energy, interactions, and circumstances. You'll live more strategically by seizing the most beneficial opportunities. With clarity of purpose and an abundance mindset, you'll release limiting beliefs and can embrace joy in every moment.

This hasn't made me softer as a businessman; it's made me even tougher. Because I have a clear purpose, I'm more certain and confident about where I'm going and how best to get there.

My persistence, coupled with my passion, translates to clear expectations for my teams. Because this comes from a place of love and because it brings me great joy even in the smallest moments, I work harder and with greater focus than ever before. I've become much more efficient and productive, developed a new rapport with my corporate teams, and driven my businesses to new heights by opening my mind to new possibilities. The irony here is that the Joy-Wealth Mindset is infinitely more suitable to facilitating maximum success than holding on to the Get-Rich and Material-Wealth Mindsets, which are riddled with limiting beliefs and ultimately lead to disappointment. Only the Joy-Wealth Mindset can empower someone to become boundless and realize their ultimate potential: being their own sultan.

# CONCLUSION

## The End Is Just the Beginning

I have one last location that I'd like to take you to before you get to the last page.

Picture us walking down a highway. The road beneath our feet represents the journey we've taken together in these chapters, exploring the way to become your own sultan and gaining dominion over your life.

When I started writing this book, I had one mission in mind: to expose readers to my philosophy that by using the Wealth Pie to balance their time and energy investments between current wealth and forecasted wealth, they can overcome the inherent limitations of the Material-Wealth Mindset and build a more fulfilling and satisfying life by adopting the Joy-Wealth Mindset instead.

Along this highway, I've shared with you my experiences and explained why the Material-Wealth Mindset is obsolete and can only promise a life that's ultimately lacking in meaning and fulfillment.

I've also shared some insights into my transformation in which I learned that no amount of material success could lead me to realize my fullest potential as the man I truly wanted to be or could offer me a life based on true wealth: joy.

Along the way, I discovered that what I really wanted was to live a life that filled me and all of those around me with an abundance of joy in every aspect of our lives. I learned that, in order to achieve that state, I must be conscious of the present, mindful of the future, and invest my time and energies in all of the myriad interests I have and want to develop.

It's been a wonderful journey for me, and I hope you've enjoyed yourself and consider our time together well spent. This portion of the journey is coming to an end now, as you can certainly tell from the few pages left to turn.

This leaves you with a decision.

Now, I've brought you to a crossroad, where our highway splits into two forks, and you must necessarily choose which one you'll continue to travel on. It's a decision you must make all on your own.

One fork will return you to the exact place where we started: the City of Expectations. You can dismiss what I've shared with you on these pages and put this book aside. As I told you from the outset, the journey of the Joy-Wealth Mindset isn't for everyone. You can put everything out of your head and rejoin the mad race for riches.

You can simply resume your place on the wheel of material wealth. You'll find that the others we've temporarily left behind will be waiting with all of the same expectations that you'll never fully satisfy and the same promise that if just keep working harder and harder, buying more and more, then one day you'll be happy.

I wouldn't blame you if that's the path you choose. That's certainly the easiest. Everything is laid out for you, and there are plenty of other people who are doing the same.

The other road is a trail that you'll have to blaze all on your own. There's no surveying crew or engineers to tell you where to go or not to go. This less-traveled path has no directions other than what you determine might lead you to your fullest personal experiences and a life filled with Joy-Wealth. There are fewer fellow travelers, no destination, and no promise of a reward at the end of the trip because the journey itself is the reward.

Every day, you'll have to get out of bed and reaffirm your determination to become the best version of yourself. You'll have to go out into the world and live with active intention. Instead of settling into the same worn routine and blindly following others, you'll have to set your mind to finding joy in all that you do and in those who surround you. There won't be a single moment in which you'll be able to coast along and follow the long line of others marching ahead of you. No, this road is uniquely your own—as is the choice.

Before you choose your course, there's one last thing I'd like to leave you with. At the beginning of this book and the start of our journey, I shared with you how much I enjoy going to the movies. It's not just the standard escapism that fuels my enthusiasm for the cinema. What I love about the movies is that they allow us to see a character at a moment in their life when they're struggling with themselves to reach their higher self. From mindless comedies to truly searing documentaries, they're all a reflection of our desire to be the ultimate versions of ourselves that we can possibly be. Maybe that's the ultimate instinctual gift from our ancestors: the drive to be the best that we can be.

I haven't made my movie ... yet! But every day, I try to lead a life that would be worthy of the screen. I want to show the audience that although I'm just a mortal man with foibles and failings—probably more than most—I'm determined to rise above these limitations and be the best man, best CEO, best husband and father, best son and friend, and best family member I can be. Every day, I face the same struggles as everyone else, but I have a main character's determination to overcome them and realize my ultimate self. Every day, I'm determined to be my own sultan.

How about you? Every one of us only gets one life in this world, and the clock is ticking for all of us. Are you making your life one that you'd want shown on a movie screen? Are you the hero of your film or merely a supporting character? Would you change that if you could?

Think of yourself as the hero of your movie. If the opening credits were running now and your character had to decide which fork in our road to take, which path would it be? What would the hero in you want to do?

Do *that.*

Whatever you eventually decide, I want you to know that this book was always intended as an introduction to my philosophy. There are supporting resources and additional content to be found on my website, and I'll be reaching out more publicly to all of those who want to continue their journey to the Joy-Wealth lifestyle.

It's your decision, of course, but I hope you'll be among them because I believe that joy is contagious. I believe that the more you adopt the Joy-Wealth Mindset and dedicate yourself to bringing joy into the world and spreading it, the more you'll create joy in the world for others. You'll be building joy exponentially.

I hope you live with the Joy-Wealth Mindset.

I hope you manifest the cinematic hero you want to be and take the first step toward living the life that leads to the ultimate version of yourself.

Most of all, I hope you strive to be your own sultan.